8-SESSION STUDY

4-R.E.A.L.

RELEVANT • ENGAGING • ALIVE • LESSONS

Real Talk for Middle and High School Youth

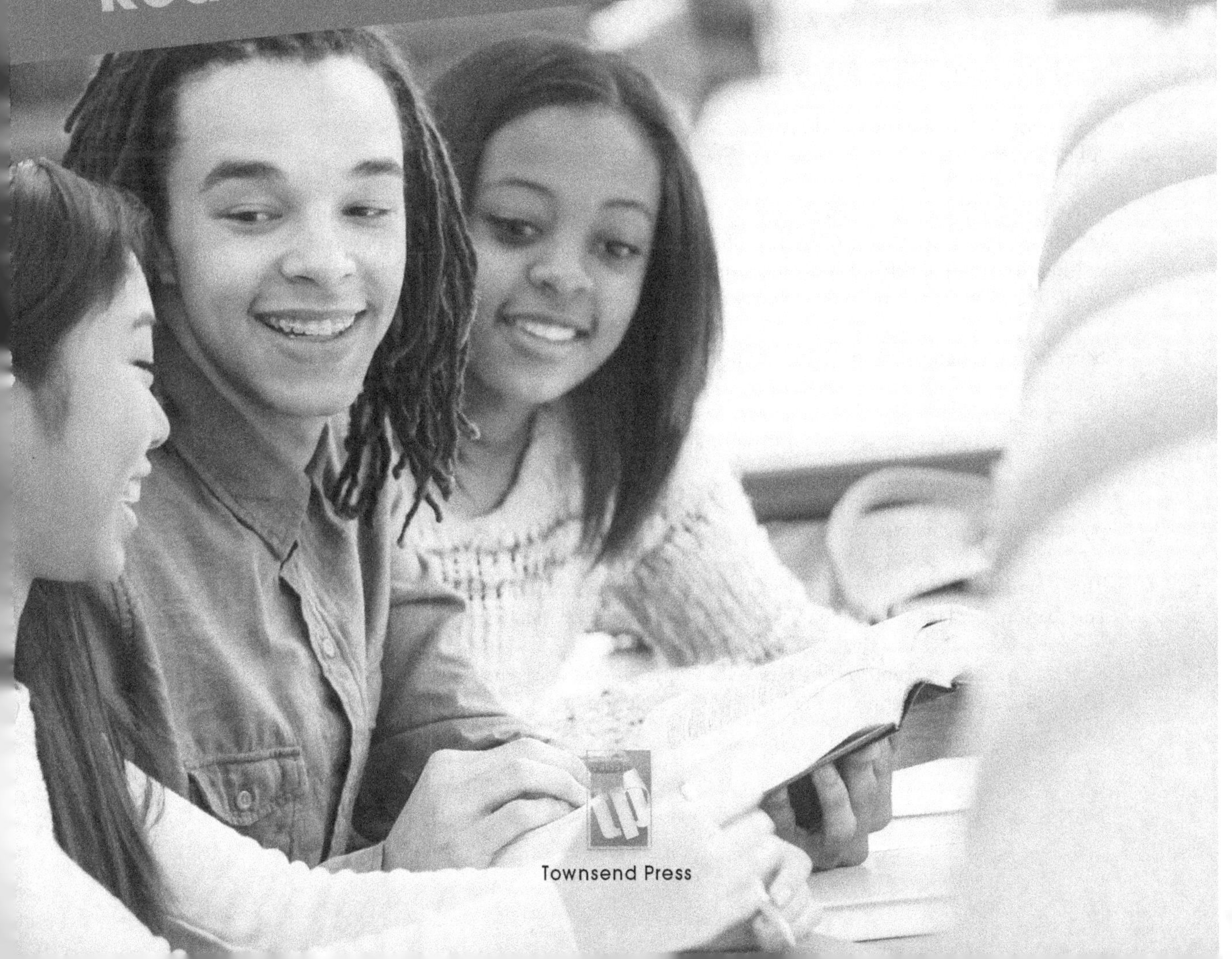

Townsend Press

4–R.E.A.L.:–Real Talk for Middle and High School Youth

Copyright © 2018 by Townsend Press
All rights reserved.

No part of this book may be reproduced or transmitted in any form, by any means, electronic or mechanical, including photocopying, recording, or by any information storage or retrieval system without the expressed permission in writing from the publisher. Permission requests may be addressed to Townsend Press, P. O. Box 70990, Nashville, Tennessee 37207-0990; or emailed to customercare@sspbnbc.com.

Scripture quotations marked KJV are from the King James Version of the Bible.

Unless otherwise noted, Scripture quotations are from the Holy Bible, NEW INTERNATIONAL VERSION® Copyright © 1973, 1978, 1984, 2011 by Biblica, Inc.® Used by permission. All rights reserved worldwide.

Those marked NKJV are taken from the New King James Version®. Copyright © 1982 by Thomas Nelson. Used by permission. All rights reserved.

Those marked NLT are from the New Living Translation copyright© 1996, 2004, 2007, 2013 by Tyndale House Foundation. Used by permission of Tyndale House Publishers Inc., Carol Stream, Illinois 60188. All rights reserved.

Scripture quotations from THE MESSAGE. Copyright © by Eugene H. Peterson 1993, 1994, 1995, 1996, 2000, 2001, 2002. Used by permission of Tyndale House Publishers, Inc.

ISBN: 978-1-949052-06-0

CONTENT

About the Author 4

Introduction 5

STUDENT LESSONS

Lesson 1   Not without Hope: The Lives of Teens in the Age of the New Millennium and Beyond 7

Lesson 2   Hope: The Expectation of Something Good 15

Lesson 3   Don't Lose Hope 23

Lesson 4   Hush! Somebody Is Calling Your Name! 31

Lesson 5   What's Your Calling? 39

Lesson 6   Setting Your Priorities by Discovering PURPOSE 47

Lesson 7   Celebrate Your Uniqueness: You Are More Important than You Realize 55

Lesson 8   Get Your Shine On! 63

FACILITATOR TIPS

Introduction to Group Facilitator Tips 71

Facilitator's Lesson Tips 73–86

About the Author

Sonya Franklin Burney is an author, educator, and professional operatic singer from Detroit, Michigan, who believes in the words of Proverbs 18:16: "A man's gift makes room for him and brings him before great men" (www.movinginmygifts.com).

Sonya attended the University of Michigan for her undergraduate years and earned two bachelor degrees in English and Music. She wrote her first book in 2004 titled *Young Warren Sings!* Her book was featured at the International Black Film Festival in 2009 in Nashville, Tennessee. She is also a professional operatic singer who has toured internationally and performed on recent and numerous occasions as a soloist with the Nashville Opera and the Nashville Symphony Chorus and Orchestra, in addition to the filmed role and performance of Marian Anderson in the operatic musical story *Portraits*, which premiered at Middle Tennessee State University in 2016. She has further upcoming performances scheduled for 2018.

In 2007, Sonya joined the Sunday School Publishing Board and during her tenure, she served as copyeditor, children's editor and youth editor. In 2013, Sonya earned a Master of Arts degree in Teaching and became a public school educator. In 2017, God blessed Sonya to complete her doctorate in educational leadership. She currently resides in Nashville, Tennessee, with her loving husband, Sgt. Jerome Burney (U.S. Army retired), and four fantastic children: Warren, Dominic, Aris, and Eva Sardon. Today, she continues her relationship with the SSPB as a freelance writer and editor of various projects. She counts it a privilege that God has allowed her to be a published author and editor of many Sunday school curricula writings and youth articles for the SSPB in order to make a difference in the lives of the youth.

Are You 4REAL?

Discrimination. Racism. School shootings. Gun control. Poverty. Same-sex marriage. Sex slavery. Orphans. Immigration. Teen drinking. Youth homicides and violence. Abortion. Persecution. Mental health. Teen health. Opioids. Methamphetamines. Marijuana. Pornography. Cyber-bullying. Social-media abuse . . .

Relevant topics such as those above seem to shadow us every day. Why are they relevant? Because you as the teenager still have to live in this type of global culture where so much of today's issues extend across lands and oceans. They can feel overwhelming and burdensome. How are you going to get the courage to stand up against all of this?

Engage and be effective. You—yes, YOU—can still engage and be effective. Don't go getting lost in your cellphones and your earbuds to hide. These issues aren't going away. Adulthood can be harder, so you may as well face it now. You need to know what's happening so that you can learn how to protect and arm yourself to fight off the high pressures every day. So now, a couple of questions: (1) Is God's Word a suggestion? (2) What if I don't know God's Word . . . now what? Don't give up; keep reading. Let's find out!

Alive and well! That would be God—and His Word. Just because you may not physically see Him or His Word doesn't mean they don't exist and are not powerful. Do you see the wind, or do you feel the effects of the wind on your face, your clothes, your hair? Just as the wind is alive, so is its Creator and His Word. If you feel dead inside, now is your chance to be alive by developing a relationship with Jesus Christ. Relationship, not religion!

Lessons learned. There's a lot to be learned. This is your book because these lessons are for you and your questions. Not your parents, grandparents, aunts, uncles—YOU. There is too much happening in the world today to waste your time. Welcome to 4–R.E.A.L.—Relevant, Engaging, and Alive Lessons that welcome "real" talk for those preteen and teenage warriors who are fighting every day with real issues that are challenges or obstacles to believing that wonder if God is real. In this book, you will learn strategies and find out who truly does fight for you. But be careful; this is a different type of battle that doesn't fit into what you might be used to seeing in this world. You may not like it at times. Or, you might get very uncomfortable. Growth feels that way sometimes. Let the lessons help you receive growth from God. Don't get caught up in all of the "crazy."

So, let's be 4–R.E.A.L. . . .

LESSON 1

Topic: Not without Hope: The Lives of Teens in the Age of the New Millennium and Beyond

(Based upon Romans 5:1-11, NIV)

Opening Prayer

Keep it real and talk to God straight from your heart. Don't pretend or worry about who is looking at you. Remember, this is your relationship with God and no one else's.

NOT WITHOUT HOPE:
The Lives of Teens in the Age of the New Millennium and Beyond

Teenagers are facing more challenges than ever before. Teen suicides, bullying, dating abuse, along with the complications of sexting, social-media Web sites, and other Internet phenomena have made the lives of teens in the new millennium quite a challenge—leaving them no hope.

How is it that anyone can keep his or her hope with so much happening in the world, and so many inappropriate exposures overwhelming teens every day? Since there is "nothing new under the sun," let's look at the role of God's Word in our lives. Can you imagine anyone having to face all these issues without knowing Jesus Christ? It is hard enough to face them when you know that you are saved, let alone without Jesus.

The problems with teens in society and in some homes today are not new. There have always been situations of teenage pregnancy, abandoned or abused teens, runaways, drugs, sexual deviances and problems, gangs, bullying, and so forth. So what is the hope?

God's Word—it never changes. It is just as powerful today as it was in past generations and it never loses power. It is alive and a living Word which brings hope to the hopeless.

We all have sinned and come short of God's standards and expectations. We are human and we make mistakes. God knew this and this is why He sent His Son to save us from a life of hopelessness and sin. What makes a saved teen different from an unsaved teen is the saved teen's knowing Jesus Christ and having the hope that each day, saved teenagers allow Jesus and His Word to make them better, because there is a greater life awaiting them in the future—giving them hope. We ask for forgiveness and eventually overcome the sin. Eventually? Yes, sometimes, when we are used to living in a certain sinful manner, it can take some practice in rejecting that lifestyle and being uncomfortable with those feelings until we are totally free. Saved teens may also experience rejection from their friends because they choose to accept Christ in their lives and His lifestyle and way of thinking—which is the only way to peace. Now, if you don't understand this example, maybe you will understand this one: does anyone like vomit? When we have been exposed to a better way of life, yet we choose to turn back to making sinful choices that will only bring us bad consequences, it is no different from a dog who chooses to eat its own vomit instead of eating what is healthy and nourishing. If your face is twisted after reading that last sentence, congratulations! Now you see the effects of what it is like in God's eyes to turn back to sin instead of turning to godly choices!

Do these kinds of godly choices lead to suffering? Yes! Expect it! When we choose Christ, we also choose the same rejection that Christ had to endure. But how did the story end for Jesus on Earth? The same way that it will end for those who choose Him—in victory! Jesus came to die for those who were in sin—or, as the Bible calls them, "the ungodly." He came to die for all of our hang-ups, mistakes, sin, craziness—whatever you wish to call it—so that we will come to know Him personally and make godly decisions based on His Word.

If you are a Christian, you will for sure have conflict in your life. At times it may seem that you have more conflict now than before you came to Christ. Be assured and joyful that God is working in your life to build you up so that you can be a real-life witness for someone else who may be going through the same problem.

There may be times when you will have to endure loneliness and cannot go to every teen event at school or in the neighborhood. Know that when this happens, it is for a reason. God has a special plan for your life that only *you* can walk out on Earth—not anyone else. Therefore, you should never compare your life to anyone else's life. When you have to endure these times in which things seem hopeless, don't give your godly plans over to teen suicide, bullying, or inappropriate Internet use. Allow yourself to be built up in God's Word by reading and studying. Get into a Bible-based youth study group and choose new friends to replace the old, sinful ones. Get your mind off yourself, and go and do something godly or helpful for someone else. Before you know it, you will be on the way to walking out God's plan for your life.

Don't give up hope! When trouble comes, it is a part of God's plan in building you up. Without both good and bad experiences, you would not be who you are today. God can take a negative situation and turn it around to make it work out for you in a blessed way. God and His Word will make you a stronger Christian, and put a driving desire to serve Him in building His kingdom. Is anyone perfect? *No!* But if you will commit your life to serve Jesus, you will never regret it, nor be the same. It is worth the ride!

So where are my gladiators? Where are the warriors? Do you have the fight in you? Once you realize your power and worth in Jesus Christ, you will have hope and be an unstoppable force for God on Earth. Your life will make a difference . . . only if you don't give up hope!

Break It Up!

"Name Tent" Icebreaker

Grab one colored piece of construction paper and a dark-colored marker. Fold the paper in half the long way. When it is opened, it should be able to stand on its own. On the outside of the name tent, clearly print your first and last name. On the back side, draw, sketch, or write three interesting aspects about yourself. They could be hobbies, likes, dislikes, and so forth. Now, at the sound of the three-minute timer, find a partner and share your work with each other.

 You can listen to music while you complete this lesson.

Trending: #notwithouthope

Essential Question

Solve this puzzle to find out the essential question of this interactive lesson.

A	B	C	D	E	F	G	H	I	J	K	L	M
1	2	3	4	5	6	7	8	9	10	11	12	13

N	O	P	Q	R	S	T	U	V	W	X	Y	Z
14	15	16	17	18	19	20	21	22	23	24	25	26

__ __ __   __ __ __   __ __ __ __ __ __ __ __ __
1 18 5   25 15 21   18 5 10 5 3 20 9 14 7

__ __ __ __ , __ __ __ __   __ __ __ __   __ __ __
 7 15 4 19   23 15 18 4   23 8 5 14   25 15 21

__ __ __ __ __ __   __ __ __ __   __ __ __ __
 3 15 13 16 1 18 5   25 15 21 18   12 9 6 5

__ __   __ __ __ __ __ __   __ __ __ __ , __ ?
20 15   19 15 13 5 14 5   5 12 19 5   19

> **Purpose**

Write a six-sentence paragraph on what the purpose is for YOU by answering this essential question of today's lesson. Are you going to answer YES or NO? Don't forget to indent. Use examples as evidence,—such as Bible verses or real-life events—to back up your position.

Here are a few other questions to consider in your answer: *Why is this important to me? How will this help me now? How will this help me later?*

_____
_____
_____
_____
_____
_____

Lesson Overview

God's Word—it never changes. It is just as powerful today as it was in past generations, and it never loses power. It is alive and a living Word that brings hope to the hopeless. God has a special plan for your life that only you—not anyone else—can perform on Earth. Therefore, you should never compare your life to anyone else's life.

Romans 5:1-11 (NIV)
1 Therefore, since we have been justified through faith, we have peace with God through our Lord Jesus Christ, **2** through whom we have gained access by faith into this grace in which we now stand. And we boast in the hope of the glory of God. **3** Not only so, but we also glory in our sufferings, because we know that suffering produces perseverance; **4** perseverance, character; and character, hope. **5** And hope does not put us to shame, because God's love has been poured out into our hearts through the Holy Spirit, who has been given to us. **6** You see, at just the right time, when we were still powerless, Christ died for the ungodly. **7** Very rarely will anyone die for a righteous person, though for a good person someone might possibly dare to die. **8** But God demonstrates his own love for us in this: While we were still sinners, Christ died for us. **9** Since we have now been justified by his blood, how much more shall we be saved from God's wrath through him! **10** For if, while we were God's enemies, we were reconciled to him through the death of his Son, how much more, having been reconciled, shall we be saved through his life! **11** Not only is this so, but we also boast in God through our Lord Jesus Christ, through whom we have now received reconciliation.

TIP—Training in Progress

The Age of the New Millennium is a world of heavy distractions. On top of the daily challenges of life that can come to all of us, add "distraction" to the top of the pile. We are distracted by the overuse of cellphones, DVR recordings, social-media sites, videos, Web sites, texting, or tweeting. Do any of these aspects bring us closer to God? How can we have hope when we are faced with so many distractions that bombard us and keep us so distracted that we develop our online lives more than our spiritual lives?

Here are a few **TIP**s:
- Pick one day out of the week for a "no cellphone" day.
- Give your cellphone to your parent/guardian before going to bed.
- Take one day not to go online to any social-media accounts.

See if your concentration or focus may start to get better. Replace the cellphone habits with other habits that will bring you closer in your relationship with Jesus. Remember this: nothing or no one in this world could ever take the place of a personal relationship with Jesus Christ.

Word Is Bond

The denotation of a word is the literal meaning or definition from the dictionary. "Context" is how a word is used in a sentence or how the words around it reveal its intended meaning.

Find a Bible and read what Romans 5:3 (NIV) says about perseverance and hope. Search an online dictionary in order to find out information about the word *perseverance*.

Find and write down the denotation of the word *perseverance*:

_____

_____

- What other words have the same meaning as *perseverance* (synonyms)?

Synonyms: _____

- What other words have the opposite meaning of *perseverance* (antonyms)?

Antonyms: _____

Context: Now, see if you can use the word *perseverance* and a synonym and one antonym of it in separate sentences.

_____

_____

_____

When you are done writing, share your sentences with three people.

Reflection 3-2-1

Share your personal reflections on the lesson today with a partner that you have not yet had the chance to work with. Write down your answers, if needed. Your answers may not be duplicated.

- Name *three* points that you recall from today's lesson.
- What *two* aspects from the lesson did you learn that you didn't know before?
- Think of *one* question that you can ask your partner regarding today's lesson.

Circle Up…

After sharing your reflections about the lesson today with your partner, each person around the circle now gets to share one reflection and explanation that was learned from the lesson.

Closing Prayer

Come together to offer a group prayer to God. Don't forget that He knows your future. If you have any concerns that need to be addressed in prayer—such as scholarship applications, college applications, an ill family member, passing any tests, understanding your school subjects, and so forth—this is the time to pray for yourself and for each other.

Inter-Action! Worksheet Activity

Socratic Seminar and Discussion

This exercise promotes critical thinking, speaking, and listening practices that are critical for today's youth. Paper, pens, and pencils will be provided.

If you have never participated in a Socratic seminar before, type this link into your browser to learn more: https://www.youtube.com/watch?v=_CPLu3qCbSU

You will now create two or three questions that will be answered in the discussion.

Examples: "What would you do if…?" or "Do you allow online activity on social-media sites to control your mood?"

1) _____

2) _____

3) _____

Here's How It Works!
Have up to six people form an inner circle. Everyone else sits outside of the circle and answers questions that those in the inner circle ask. Only the people in the inner circle can ask questions; however, they cannot give any answers. Again, only those who sit outside of the circle can give answers. These answers must be biblically based.

LESSON 2

Topic: Hope: The Expectation of Something Good
(Based upon Jeremiah 29, NIV)

Opening Prayer

Keep it real and talk to God straight from your heart. Don't pretend or worry about who is looking at you. Remember, this is your relationship with God and no one else's.

HOPE:
The Expectation of Something Good

HOPE IS SIMPLY DEFINED AS "THE EXPECTATION OF SOMETHING GOOD." It may represent the way one views and responds to his/her experiences in life. One may either see life as the glass being half-empty, or the glass being half-full. Or one may view times of trouble as barriers—preventing progress or opportunities to enhance growth and display characteristics such as determination, strength, and courage. Being hopeful can be a state of mind—the attitude one possesses as she/he approaches various situations in life.

Author and motivational speaker Zig Ziglar stated, "Your attitude, not your aptitude, will determine your altitude." This statement simply means that one's attitude (not solely his/her ability) will determine how far he/she goes in life. There is also another statement that you have either heard or even said: "I'm not going to get my hopes up." This statement sounds a bit negative—and it may even be a valid sentiment—but it also serves another purpose. This statement often serves to keep one from becoming disappointed if/when things do not work out the way he/she thought they would. It becomes a way for one to protect himself/herself from the pain of feeling rejected, experiencing a sense of failure, or being the victim of someone's failed promises. Such a statement is often referred to as a coping mechanism that helps people deal with the failures in their lives. Many youth approach the sentiment of this statement as a coping mechanism because of the negative conditions that they face in life.

As a youth in today's society, you are growing up in a financially unstable environment where the unemployment rate is the highest it has ever been, especially among people of color. The public education system continues to fall short of academically preparing youth for success and is more consumed with policing youth than with educating them. Poverty has increased and alongside of that, violence has become a normal way to survive another day. Adults who are supposed to love and protect youth are the very ones who not only emotionally, physically, and sexually abuse them, but also abandon and neglect them; and, consequently, some youth are placed in a juvenile facility or an inadequate foster-care system. Then when some youth dream of going to either college or a vocational school, it has become a more distant reality—as the cost of tuition continues to rise and funding is less available to those who need financial assistance. This list is very discouraging and helps to explain why some youth may say, "Don't get your hopes up." Some youth live in a present reality that is stagnating instead of progressing.

Have no fear . . . there is a place for renewed hope, but it rests neither in society nor in institutions, but in a God who encourages us by His words to the prophet Jeremiah: "'For I know the plans I have for you,' says the LORD. 'They are plans for good and not for disaster, to give you a future and a hope'" (Jeremiah 29:11, NLT). In order to understand the importance of this verse, one must remember who said it. God said it and God is powerful and is in control of this world and what happens in society. We must remember that we are talking about a God who, just by speaking, created the world in six days and managed *everything*. God is truly in control and is able to do the impossible. God declares in Jeremiah 32:27, "I am the LORD, the God of all the peoples of the world. Is anything too hard for me?" (NLT).

There is nothing too hard for God, which is why we do not have to lose hope. In fact, God is our hope—so in our merely considering every negative item previously listed, we must conclude that there is nothing on that list that is too hard for God to work out for us. In other words, instead of focusing so much on the problem which seems like a mountain, why not turn that focus onto God, who can solve the problem and provide us with the strength to overcome? By our taking this view, troubles and problems may be viewed in an entirely new way, instead of seeing them as problems; they become possibilities for God's presence and power in our lives.

Now, of course, we each have a part to play as well, because in Jeremiah 29:12-14a, God states, "'In those days when you pray, I will listen. If you look for me wholeheartedly, you will find me. I will be found by you,' says the LORD" (NLT). There must be some action that we take—and that means talking to God and asking God to work on our behalf while we do all that we can do. God loves us and will do it. Now we must remind ourselves that this does not mean that the problem will go away or that we should deny that the problem even exists; what it does mean is that we may view it in a way where we can expect that something good will come from the situation. Life does contain disappointments, but our having an attitude of hope opens us up to the possibilities of what God will accomplish in our lives. Life may disappoint, but the Bible encourages us that God will not disappoint. How do we know that God will not disappoint? God told us so by stating in Isaiah 49:23c, "Those who hope in me will not be disappointed." Now that is something we can hope for!

Break It Up!

"Name Tent" Icebreaker

As instructed by your teacher, help form a circle, either standing or sitting. Based upon the name-tent activity from the previous lesson, let's see how many names and personal points you can remember about your classmates. The person with the most correct information will win a prize from the teacher.

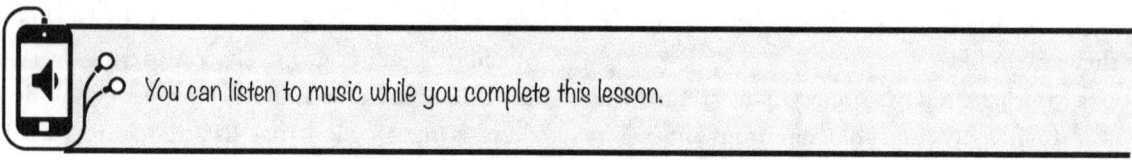

You can listen to music while you complete this lesson.

Trending: #greatexpectations

Essential Question

Unscramble the word order of this essential question for this interactive lesson. When you have the answer, write it down on the line below.

GOD HARD THERE ANYTHING IS FOR TOO?

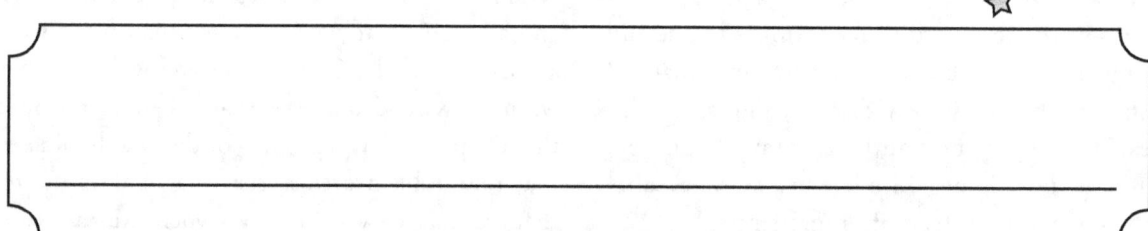

Purpose

Do you think you know the answer to this question? Write down one six-sentence paragraph on what the purpose is for YOU by answering this essential question of today's lesson. Don't forget to indent. Use examples as evidence (such as Bible verses or real-life examples) to back up your position. Here are a few other questions to consider in your answer: *Why is this important to me? How will this help me now? How will this help me later?*

_____
_____
_____
_____
_____
_____

Lesson Overview

God is truly in control and is able to do the impossible. God declares in Jeremiah 32:27, "I am the LORD, the God of all the peoples of the world. Is anything too hard for me?" (NLT).

There is nothing too hard for God, which is why we do not have to lose hope. In fact, God is our hope; we must conclude that there is nothing that is too hard for God to work out for us.

Jeremiah 32:27 (NIV)
27 "I am the LORD, the God of all mankind. Is anything too hard for me?"

TIP—Training in Progress

The Age of the New Millennium is not only a world of heavy distractions, but will leave you with very little hope of anything getting better. Where do you place your hope? Do you hope in humans? Money? Education? Degrees? Social connections? Friends? Family? Can any of these areas bring us closer to God? Or do they drive us farther away from Him? Think about the last time you became discouraged in someone or something. What did you do to regain your hope?

Here are some **TIP**s:

- Use an Internet search engine to find Scriptures about hope.
- Write down the similarities and differences between expectations and having hope. Do you find that maybe your expectations are reasonable or unreasonable?
- How does hope relate to keeping promises, trust, and faith? Or does it relate at all?
- Redefine who or what is worthy of having your hope.

Put your hope in God and His Word.

Word Is Bond

The denotation of a word means the literal meaning or definition from the dictionary. "Context" means how the word is used in a sentence, or vocabulary words that are used in context.

Use an online dictionary in order to find out the following information about the words *expectation* and *hope*.

Find and write down the denotations of the words *expectation* and *hope*.

_____

_____

- What other words have the same meaning as *expectation* (synonyms)?

Synonyms: _____

- What other words have the opposite meaning of *expectation* (antonyms)?

Antonyms: _____

Context: Now, see if you can use the word *expectation* and one synonym and one antonym of it in sentences.

_____

_____

When you are done writing, go and find three different people with whom to share your sentences with to see if their sentences match up to your own!

- What other words have the same meaning as *hope* (synonyms)?

Synonyms: _____

- What other words have the opposite meaning of *hope* (antonyms)?

Antonyms: _____

Context: Now, see if you can use the word *hope* and one synonym and one antonym of it in sentences.
_____
_____

Can you find other words in other languages (like Spanish, Italian, French, etc.) that mean the same as *hope*?

Reflection 3-2-1

Find a partner with whom to discuss what you learned in today's lesson. Write down your answers, if needed. Your answers may not be duplicated.
- Name *three* points that you recall from today's lesson.
- What *two* aspects from the lesson did you learn that you didn't know before?
- Think of *one* question that you can ask your partner regarding today's lesson.

Circle Up...

After forming a circle with your classmates, each student should go around the circle and express one expectation of hope that they have of God's power in their lives.

Closing Prayer

Come together to offer a group prayer to God. Don't forget that He knows your future. If you have any concerns that need to be addressed in prayer—such as scholarship applications, college applications, an ill family member, passing any tests, understanding your school subjects, and so forth—this is the time to pray for yourself and for each other. Remember to always have hope in God.

Inter-Action! Worksheet Activity

Vision Board

As you already know from Jeremiah 29:11, God has a plan to prosper you in all areas of your life. Submit all your plans to God so that He can direct you to the right people and places at the right time. Don't worry about what other people are doing who don't serve God and seem to get away with it. They will eventually have to face consequences on their own.

Do the following as a class:

- Decide on three biblical Scriptures that will give direction, focus, and guidance to build and support your expectations. (Example: These expectations could be to become more comfortable with using the Bible, to memorizing and meditating on Scriptures, to surrounding yourself with more godly friends who support the Christian lifestyle.)
- Select a construction board of an agreed color.
- Get glue, scissors, and magazine pictures.
- Make it creative and fun!
- Post it in your classroom and watch your expectations and hopes come true when you work and put effort into your goals!

Visit this Web site for ideas on how to create a vision board: https://blog.mindvalley.com/vision-board/?utm_source=google_blog.

LESSON 3

Topic: Don't Lose Hope
(Based upon the book of Habakkuk, NIV)

🙏 Opening Prayer

Keep it real and talk to God straight from your heart. Don't pretend or worry about who is looking at you. Remember, this is your relationship with God and no one else's.

DON'T LOSE HOPE

SOMETIMES IT SEEMS AS THOUGH THE PEOPLE WHO DO THE MOST WRONG ARE THE SAME PEOPLE WHO ARE LIVING THE GLAMOROUS LIFE. Some actors do immoral things and some rappers readily use profanity, yet they have all the money and fame that anyone could want. Some celebrities drive the most expensive cars, live in the most lavish homes, and vacation in the most beautiful places—yet some of them are mean to the people around them, and some abuse their bodies with drugs and alcohol. It certainly does not seem like they are reaping what they have sown. This observation doesn't just apply to celebrities, though. In school, you might notice that the starting quarterback can miss class and be late for practice, yet never gets punished. Or you may have a younger sibling who can get away with everything that your parents yelled at you about when you were his/her age. It can be frustrating to see people getting away with doing the wrong thing!

The Bible says that the wicked will be punished and that judgment will come to those who do wrong. But it never seems like the judgment happens; the people getting away with wrong just keep getting rewarded, while those who are doing the right thing get ignored. The prophet Habakkuk complained to God about a similar situation (see Habakkuk 1). Habakkuk saw that his people were suffering—but even worse, they were suffering at the hands of people who were evil. Habakkuk cried out to God and asked for something to be done to save his people from their suffering and from the attacks of the Babylonians—but God seemed to remain silent. Habakkuk struggled to understand how an almighty God would allow His people to be overtaken by an evil nation. You could imagine how frustrated and discouraged Habakkuk must have been!

When we find ourselves in similar situations as that of the prophet Habakkuk's, and frustration and discouragement set in, we can be tempted to do a couple of things. First, we may be tempted to wish for wicked things to happen to wicked people. Most people just want life to be fair, and for everyone to get what they deserve; but there is a fine line between justice and vengeance. Justice has to do with what is fair and reasonable for everyone, while vengeance is punishment in return for a wrong. Justice is communal; vengeance is personal. When someone gets away with doing the wrong thing, we sometimes take it personally—as though the person did something to purposely hurt us. Chances are that the person we want to see go down meant no direct harm to us at all.

In order to avoid being vengeful toward others, we must remember that there were times when we ourselves did not do the right thing, yet God did not punish us. The Bible tells us that God is merciful and kind, and gives people every chance they need to come into the knowledge of Christ. It is not cool for us to want someone to get caught doing wrong just so we can feel better, yet want God to show us mercy when we do wrong. Second, we can be tempted to change teams. It can seem foolish to try to do everything the Bible says when it does not seem to get any positive results. It may seem like there are a lot of things that we as Christians miss out on because of our faith—where we still may not be seeing any of the benefits of our sacrifices. It is tempting to just start doing what everyone else is doing, because they seem to have all the fun and none of the worries. It is in times like these that we have to remain hopeful. Even though it may not seem like things are going the way they are supposed to go and the wrong people are getting the best things, we must remain hopeful that God will make things right.

The book of Habakkuk tells us about a major problem that comes along with people who seem to get away with evil all the time: they tend to believe their own hype. In Habakkuk 1:11, the Bible says that the Babylonians' strength was their god. They idolized their army, fighting skills, and strength. In the end, we find out that those things mean very little and can be taken away so easily. People who place their hope in temporary things, and make earthly things their god, are setting themselves up for a major collapse.

As Christians, our hope should not be rooted in how big of a house we live in, or what brand of clothes we are wearing. As Christians, our faith, trust, and hope should be in God. There will be plenty of times when things do not seem fair, and it seems like good people have the worst luck. We have to be careful not to let frustration and discouragement take away our hope. God truly does see all the right things we do and all the good decisions we make. God also sees all the bad things we do and bad decisions we make (as well as the ones made by others). When the time is right, everything will balance out in our lives just the way it needs to.

Break It Up!

How Do You Spell HOPE?

On a sheet of paper, create an acrostic of the word HOPE. For example: H is for Heaven. When you are finished, share your acrostics with each other.

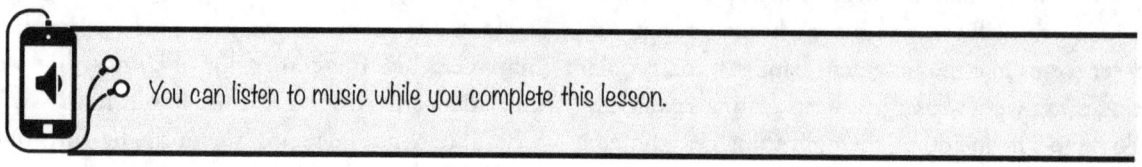

You can listen to music while you complete this lesson.

Trending: #restorationhope

Essential Question

What do you know or want to know or learn about the restoration of hope?

Purpose

In the previous lessons, you have been asked to write a reflective paragraph on the essential question for the lesson. This time, work with a partner and make a chart with three columns that are labeled "K," "W," and "L" for "What do you **K**now or **W**ant to know about or **L**earn" about this essential question. Discuss the question with your partner first. Then, both of you list your answers under the columns. Leave the "L" column blank because you will fill that in at the end of the lesson. Use Bible verses or real-life situations as examples.

K	W	L

Lesson Overview

As Christians, our faith, trust, and hope should be in God.

There will be plenty of times when things do not seem fair, and it seems like good people have the worst luck. We have to be careful not to let frustration and discouragement take away our hope.

God truly does see all the right things we do and all the good decisions we make. God also sees all the bad things we do and bad decisions we make (as well as the ones made by others). When the time is right, everything will balance out in our lives just the way it needs to.

> **Habukkah 1:2-11 (NIV)**
> **2** How long, Lord, must I call for help, but you do not listen? Or cry out to you, "Violence!" but you do not save? **3** Why do you make me look at injustice? Why do you tolerate wrongdoing? Destruction and violence are before me; there is strife, and conflict abounds. **4** Therefore the law is paralyzed, and justice never prevails. The wicked hem in the righteous, so that justice is perverted. **5** "Look at the nations and watch—and be utterly amazed. For I am going to do something in your days that you would not believe, even if you were told. **6** I am raising up the Babylonians, that ruthless and impetuous people, who sweep across the whole earth to seize dwellings not their own. **7** They are a feared and dreaded people; they are a law to themselves and promote their own honor. **8** Their horses are swifter than leopards, fiercer than wolves at dusk. Their cavalry gallops headlong; their horsemen come from afar. They fly like an eagle swooping to devour; **9** they all come intent on violence. Their hordes advance like a desert wind and gather prisoners like sand. **10** They mock kings and scoff at rulers. They laugh at all fortified cities; by building earthen ramps they capture them. **11** Then they sweep past like the wind and go on—guilty people, whose own strength is their god."

TIP—Training in Progress

If there is restoration of hope, that means at one point hope was lost or discouraged. Think about the last time you became discouraged in someone or something. What did you do to regain your hope? How did you restore your hope in someone else who may have lost it due to the death of a loved one, the loss of a job, divorce, and so forth?

Here are some **TIPs**:
- List different experiences that could make a person become hopeless. This will start the building of empathy for those who do not have hope. Empathy is when a person identifies with what someone else may feel or experience in a certain situation.

- One of the quickest ways to move out of hopelessness is to serve others. There is joy in serving others, and it can restore a person's faith in the love of God.
- How does hope relate to keeping promises, trust, and faith? Or does it?
- Having hope in a thing or outcome means there is an investment happening. Where are you investing your hope?

Word Is Bond

The denotation of a word means the literal meaning or definition from the dictionary. "Context" means how that word is used in a sentence, or vocabulary words that are used in a way that reveal their meaning.

Use an online dictionary to find out the following information about the word *restore*.

Find and write down the denotation of the word *restore*.

_____

_____

- What other words have the same meaning as *restore* (synonyms)?

Synonyms: _____

- What other words have the opposite meaning of *restore* (antonyms)?

Antonyms: _____

Context: Now, see if you can use the word *restore* and a synonym and an antonym of it in sentences.

_____

_____

When you are done writing, share your sentences with three people.

Reflection 3-2-1

Share your personal reflections on the lesson today with a selected partner that you have not yet had the chance to work with.

Find a partner with whom to discuss what you learned in today's lesson. Your answers may not be duplicated.

- Name *three* things you recall about today's lesson.
- What *two* aspects from the lesson did you learn that you didn't know before?
- Think of *one* question that you can ask your partner regarding today's lesson.

Circle Up...

After sharing your reflections about the lesson today with your partner, both of you now should fill in the "L" column of the KWL chart that you started and worked on earlier. Count how many more aspects you have learned and written down now as compared to the beginning of the lesson.

Form a circle with your classmates, then take turns expressing one expectation of hope that you have of God's power in your life.

Closing Prayer

Come together to offer a group prayer to God. Don't forget that He knows your future. If you have any concerns that need to be addressed in prayer—such as scholarship applications, college applications, an ill family member, passing any tests, understanding your school subjects, and so forth—this is the time to pray for yourself and for each other. Remember to always have hope in God.

Inter-Action! Worksheet Activity

You Can Restore Hope

Sometimes, when people lose hope they lose their joy. They might feel that there are too many things happening that are out of their control. But are we really in control in the first place? One way that a person can regain hope is to take the time to serve others and not dwell on the problem. God is so much bigger than our problems.

Together as a class, come up with a service project out in the community that you will do for the next two class meetings. Check with your teacher and decide upon two reputable organizations with whom your class can do community/volunteer service. If your church has a community or volunteer event coming up, find out if your class can help. If not, ask your teacher or another trusted adult from your church to make the arrangements for your class to serve in the community and restore hope through serving others.

LESSON 4

Topic: Hush! Somebody Is Calling Your Name!
(Based upon Isaiah 43:1; Jeremiah 1:5, NIV)

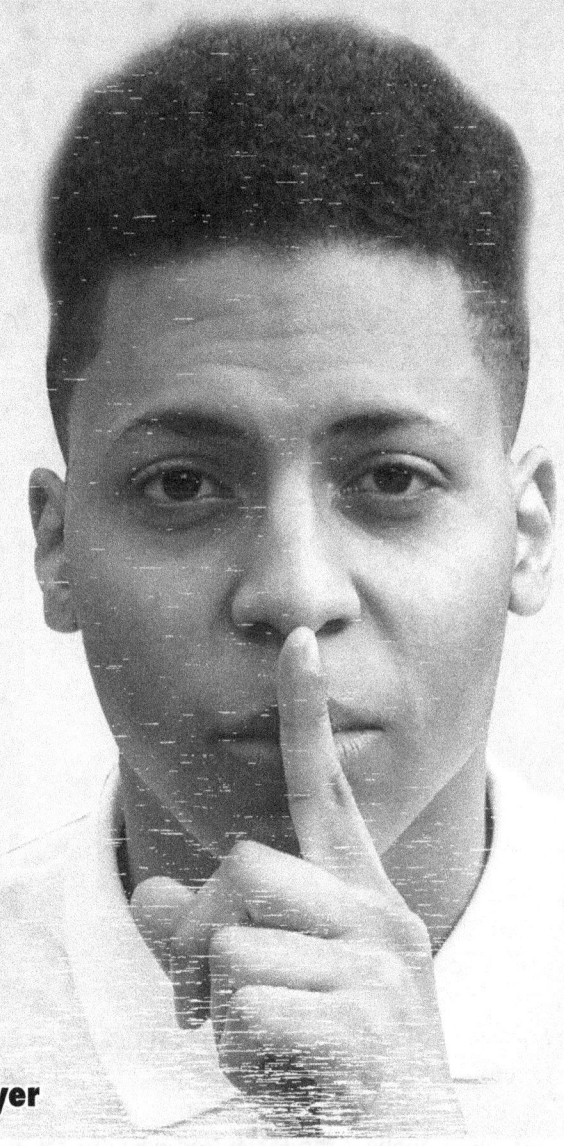

Opening Prayer

Keep it real and talk to God straight from your heart. Don't pretend or worry about who is looking at you. Remember, this is your relationship with God and no one else's.

HUSH!
Somebody Is Calling Your Name!

Have you ever been in a situation where you just did not know the answer? Sweaty palms, cotton mouth, degrading thoughts, and anger. The teacher calls your name and . . . nothing. Believe it or not, you are not the first person this has happened to. In the "class of life," all throughout the Bible, God called many people and sometimes in response all that came out was fear, anger, and maybe a thought of obedience (but mostly rebellion). The tasks that God gives always seem impossible. Throughout these lessons, we see how God's people feel when asked to do the impossible. So, the question for you is, are you ready to answer when God calls?

God Knows Your Name

God is still calling people today, but it can be hard to hear the voice of God if we don't understand how God operates. Every time God called a person, He called him or her by name. Isn't that cool? God knows your name! Isaiah 43:1 tells us that He even knows our names because He created us and He redeemed us when Jesus died on the Cross for our sins. God does not just know your name because He is cool with your parents; God knows the name that He gave you when He created you. This is the name that God uses to call you. Just like Paul, it is hard for us to respond to God when we don't know how God addresses us. God calls us to do His work, but we cannot begin to obey when God cannot get our attention. Know your God-given name and answer the call by working in your spiritual gifts and qualities.

Ordinary People Doing the Extraordinary!

"Before you saw the light of day, I had holy plans for you" (Jeremiah 1:5b, MSG). Living everyday life (school, sports, etc.) can make us seem as though we ourselves are preparing for our own lives. When God calls us, He takes our game plan, rips it up, and lays out a new plan. Everything needed was already inside the person that God called. When God called the people of the Bible to serve, they were not famous or known for anything. Some of whom God called in the Bible were runaways like Moses, or regular working people like Gideon. However, these ordinary people became leaders of nations and known to generations today. Jeremiah 1:5a tells us that God says, "Before I shaped you in the womb, I knew all about you" (MSG). Before you were even placed on this Earth God had a plan for you. God knows what we are capable of because God provided it.

Mission Impossible Turns Possible

From the Old Testament to the New Testament, the Bible is filled with stories of common people doing strange, impossible tasks. Imagine a dodgeball game where God is the captain. Instead of choosing the seemingly "good" players, God chooses the quietest, smallest, and most unconfident people on the face of the earth, and He uses them. God's call is always unpredictable and unique. God will never request a mass of volunteers but He talks directly to whomever He has gifted to work. Noah was an ordinary man when God gave him a unique order to build an ark in a desert where it never rained. But through obedience, Noah honored God and God gave him everything he needed to survive.

Have You Been Called?

God is calling your name—get excited! Believe it or not, God is still performing supernatural miracles through ordinary people every day. In order to hear God calling, you have to know your name and know your value in Him to complete the task. The task may seem impossible, but like He had done with Jeremiah, God will give you the words, actions, and confidence to make the impossible possible. Being obedient to God's call is always worth the sacrifice of comfort!

"Hush, somebody is calling your name!"

Break It Up!

Take one note card from your teacher and keep it until the end of today's lesson.

What are Negro spirituals? Have you ever heard of them? Read and listen to the information found at this link to find out more information: https://www.loc.gov/item/ihas.200197495/.

 You can listen to music while you complete this lesson.

Trending: #Godknowsmyname

Essential Question

Do you know what to do when God calls your name?

Purpose

 What's in a name? Use an Internet search engine to look up popular boy and girl names for babies. When we are born, what we are named is important because names serve to identify who we are in the world. Names have meaning. See if you can find the meaning of your name or a name that is similar, and relate the meaning of your name to the purpose of your life.

Lesson Overview

God is still calling people today, but it can be hard to hear the voice of God if we don't understand how God operates. Every time God called a person, He called him or her by name. Isn't that cool? God knows your name! Isaiah 43:1 tells us that He even knows our names because He created us and He redeemed us when Jesus died on the Cross for our sins. God does not just know your name because He is cool with your parents; God knows the name that He gave you when He created you. This is the name that God uses to call you. Just like Paul, it is hard for us to respond to God when we don't know how God addresses us. God calls us to do His work, but we cannot begin to obey when God cannot get our attention. Know your God-given name and answer the call by working in your spiritual gifts and qualities.

Isaiah 43:1 (NIV)
1 But now, this is what the LORD says—he who created you, Jacob, he who formed you, Israel: "Do not fear, for I have redeemed you; I have summoned you by name; you are mine."

Jeremiah 1:5 (NIV)
5 "Before I formed you in the womb I knew you, before you were born I set you apart; I appointed you as a prophet to the nations."

TIP—Training in Progress

Please understand that just as God knows your name, so does the enemy. Be careful of your name and the reputation that comes with it. Persons' reputations can either help or destroy them with other people. Make sure that you do all that you can to live a godly life and make a godly name for yourself.

Here are some **TIP**s:

- Not everyone that knows your name has godly intentions. Be careful!

- God knows everything about you and has purpose for your life.

- Though it may feel like you are forgotten, God knows your name even in the worst of times.

- The Holy Spirit has been described as having a still, small voice. You may be called to fulfill a special calling or action, when you least expect it, to bless someone else.

- It is important that we break away from all distractions like people, activities, cellphones, and television to become silent and still so that we can hear God's call.

- Always listen for God's voice.

Word Is Bond

 An *epithet* is a brief, descriptive phrase that helps to characterize a specific person or objet. Thousands of years ago, including the biblical times, epithets were used to describe a person, their reputation, and their bloodline.

The denotation of a word means the literal meaning or definition from the dictionary. "Context" means how the word is used in a sentence, or vocabulary words that are used in a way that reveals their meaning.

Use an online dictionary to find out the following information about the word *epithet*.

Find and write down the denotation of the word *epithet*:

_____

_____

- What other words have the same meaning as *epithet* (synonyms)?

Synonyms: _____

- What other words have the opposite meaning of *epithet* (antonyms)?

Antonyms: _____

Context: Now, see if you can use the word *epithet* and a synonym and an antonym of it in sentences.

_____

_____

When you are done writing, share your sentences with three people to see if their sentences match with your own!

Can you find words in other languages (like Greek, Latin, Spanish, Italian, or French) that mean the same as *epithet*?

Reflection 3-2-1

Find a partner with whom to discuss what you learned in today's lesson. Write down your answers, if needed. Your answers may not be duplicated.

- Name *three* points that you recall about today's lesson.
- What *two* aspects from the lesson did you learn that you didn't know before?
- Think of *one* question that you can ask your partner regarding today's lesson.

Circle Up...

Write your answers to the following questions on the index card that you received at the beginning of the lesson:

(1) What is a Negro spiritual, and what does it have to do with today's lesson?

(2) Why is listening for God's voice important?

(3) What is the big deal about a name?

(4) Will you know what to do when God calls your name?

Now, share your answers together as a class.

Closing Prayer

Come together to offer a group prayer to God. Don't forget that He knows your future. If you have any concerns that need to be addressed in prayer—such as scholarship applications, college applications, an ill family member, passing any tests, understanding your school subjects, and so forth—this is the time to pray for yourself and for each other. Remember that God knows your name and never forgets about you.

Inter-Action! Worksheet Activity

Create Your Own Epithet
Collaborative Poster

What is an epithet? An *epithet* is a brief, descriptive phrase that helps to characterize a particular person or object.

Take some time to think about what your most important characteristics are and how you would best describe yourself. Turn those characteristics into brief, descriptive phrases about yourself. Write the phrases on the lines below.

Here is a list of guidelines for making your own unique epithet:

- Include three descriptive and creative epithets about you.

- Use creative, specific, descriptive phrases that highlight the significance of these personality characteristics.

- Include pictures or graphics to illustrate your descriptions.

- Be neat! Use white paper or construction paper for your work. You all will make a collage of your work on poster or butcher paper as a class to be posted on the wall.

Here's a couple of general examples of an epithet. Now, you make yours to describe your life:

MOM
Worker of [*job*]
Courageous mother of children
Taker of vacations or stay-cations

DAD
Spectator of football
Payer of bills
Snorer to the pillows

_____

_____

_____

LESSON 5

Topic: What's Your Calling?
(Based upon Exodus 3–4, NIV)

Opening Prayer

Keep it real and talk to God straight from your heart. Don't pretend or worry about who is looking at you. Remember, this is your relationship with God and no one else's.

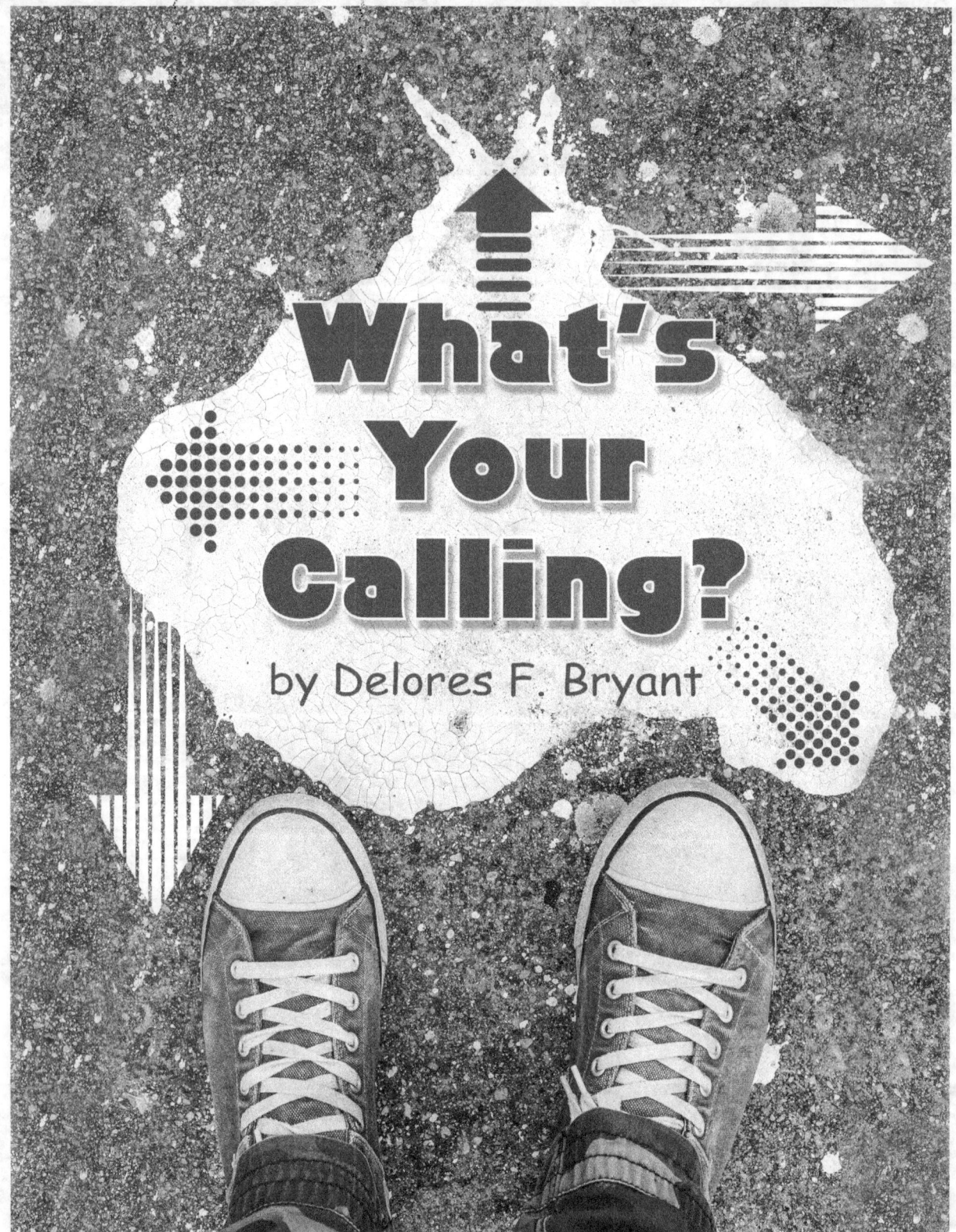

The Creator of all things, who guides and leads us toward His promises, calls us to seek Him daily during good times and in bad times. When we seek God daily, we receive the directions needed toward the choices in our lives. As youth, you may have decided to do your best in school so that you can graduate from high school and then go on to college. How did you come to the conclusion that you would pursue college or even a training program? Did you have some special experience that caused you to think on pursuing college, or were you influenced by a family member or loved one? Perhaps the calling experiences that Moses (and other prophets like Jeremiah, Ezekiel, or even Amos) had can help you in your decision making.

Moses was one chosen by God to perform a major task, but he did not think he could handle the job assignment. The angel of the Lord appeared to Moses through the midst of a burning bush—the bush that was not consumed by the fire—and got Moses' attention. Then God spoke to Moses, saying the following:

> "So now, go. I am sending you to Pharaoh to bring my people the Israelites out of Egypt." . . . God said, "I will be with you. And this will be the sign to you that it is I who have sent you: When you have brought the people out of Egypt, you will worship God on this mountain." (Exodus 3:10, 12)

This was a direct instruction to Moses of what to do, but it also provided an assurance that God would be with him throughout the process. God will be with you in whatever you are going through, just like He was with Moses. Note that Moses thought he was unable to speak, because of his speech impairment. In Exodus 4:10 (KJV), Moses said, "O my Lord, I am not eloquent, neither heretofore, nor since thou hast spoken unto thy servant: but I am slow of speech, and of a slow tongue."

So God sent Moses some help through Aaron. When Moses would speak, Aaron was the spokesperson because Moses had a deficiency in speaking. But that's what God will do for you: He will send you some help during your difficult times, just like He did for Moses. Instead of not following the will of God, and acting on an instruction from God, remember that God will send you some help.

If it is the will of God for you to go to school and graduate from a college, you need to know that God will help you along the way. When you begin to think that you are defeated, just like Moses felt, know that help is on the way. God will deliver and then you will be successful. Just as Moses was successful in delivering the children out of the hands of Pharaoh, God will deliver you—just in time. You just have to follow His instruction; you should study the path of God. There may not be a burning-bush experience as Moses' had, but you will and can explore the path toward God so you will have an assurance of His will for your life. Study the Word of God, learn of God, study the passages of Scripture from biblical days, and along the way you will be assured of God's direction for your life, and you will know His will for your life, and success will be yours—just as it was for Moses. You will know who called you, and you will know what you are commissioned to do. Know the calling for your life!

Break It Up!

Simon Says . . . Really!

You are getting ready to play a game called "Simon Says" that deals with listening and receiving instructions. One person is chosen to be Simon; the others are the players. Leading the group, Simon tells players what they must do. However, the players must only obey directions that begin with the words "Simon says." For example, if Simon says, "Simon says touch your chin," then players must touch their chin. The point is to listen and receive instructions, and follow directions. What would you do if "God says…"?

You can listen to music while you complete this lesson.

Trending: #Godiscallingyou

Essential Question

Do you know what to do when God calls your name?

Purpose

Many teens struggle with figuring out why they were created. God knows your calling, and it is tied to your purpose. "A man's gift makes room for him, and brings him before great men" (Proverbs 18:16, NKJV). Usually, when our names are called by our parents/guardians and teachers, it is attached with directions right after it. Do you answer them and complete the task immediately, or maybe you give a slow response depending on who is calling you and what you think the task is at hand to perform? Even worse, some teens ignore them when they are calling. Many teens have cellphones with caller ID and contacts so that they know who is trying to reach them. If it is an unknown number, usually people don't answer the call. Oddly, there may be some people that do call, and the receiver of the call may choose to ignore the call by not answering. The call usually goes to voicemail, and the person can check the message later. Answer the call of God on your life!

Lesson Overview

Study the Word of God, learn of God, study the passages of Scripture from biblical days, and along the way you will be assured of God's direction for your life. You will also know His will for your life, and success will be yours—just as it was for Moses. You will know who called you, and you will know what you are commissioned to do. Know the calling for your life!

> **Exodus 3:10, 12 (NIV)**
> 10 "So now, go. I am sending you to Pharaoh to bring my people the Israelites out of Egypt."
> . . . . .
> 12 God said, "I will be with you. And this will be the sign to you that it is I who have sent you: When you have brought the people out of Egypt, you will worship God on this mountain."

TIP—Training in Progress

Here are some **TIP**s:

- Don't ignore the calling of God. When He calls, answer immediately through action.
- God knows everything about you and has a purpose for your life.
- Your task is meant just for you to complete and no one else.
- Follow God's directions for the task(s) that you must complete.
- What are you passionate about?
- Exercise your talents. It could be music, writing, speaking, cooking, cleaning, etc.
- Sometimes, tasks will change.
- Always listen for God's call.

Word Is Bond

 The denotation of a word means the literal meaning or definition from the dictionary. "Context" means how the word is used in a sentence, or vocabulary words that are used in a way that reveals their meaning.

Use an online dictionary to find out the following information about the word *tenacious*.

Find and write down the denotation of the word *tenacious*:

_____

_____

- What other words have the same meaning as *tenacious* (synonyms)?

Synonyms: _____

- What other words have the opposite meaning of *tenacious* (antonyms)?

Antonyms: _____

Context: Now, see if you can use the word *tenacious* and a synonym and an antonym of it in sentences.

_____

_____

When you are done writing, share your sentences with three people to see if their sentences match with your own!

Can you find words in other languages (like Greek, Latin, Spanish, Italian, or French) that mean the same as *tenacious*?

Reflection 3-2-1

Share your personal reflections on the lesson today with a selected partner that you have not yet had the chance to work with.

Find a partner with whom to discuss what you learned in today's lesson. Write down your answers, if needed. Your answers may not be duplicated.

- Name *three* points that you recall about today's lesson.
- What *two* aspects from the lesson did you learn that you didn't know before?
- Think of *one* question that you can ask your partner regarding today's lesson.

Circle Up...

Four Corners

There are four areas in your room that have either a large Post-it® note or blank paper taped to the wall. Each of them contains one of the labels "Strongly Agree," or "Agree," "Disagree," or "Strongly Disagree." You will hear statements about the lesson today dealing with hope and expectations. When the teacher has read them aloud, decide what your answer is, and then move in front of one of the areas listed on the wall. For example, when you hear "I know that God has a plan for my life," choose your response and then stand in front of the statement that reflects your opinion.

Closing Prayer

Come together to offer a group prayer to God. Don't forget that He knows your future. If you have any concerns that need to be addressed in prayer—such as scholarship applications, college applications, an ill family member, passing any tests, understanding your school subjects, and so forth—this is the time to pray for yourself and for each other. There is a call on your life to be a living example of God's Word.

Inter-Action! Worksheet Activity

Find the vocabulary words listed below that relate to living out the purpose of God's calling. Take some time to discover their definitions and meanings.

```
E G T N E R E V E R I V W V M
P R M J M O B P F R S E L J Z
V W B P O R W U T N E D U R P
G I N S T R U C T I O N M Y T
O D L U F T C A T X P K N H E
M N D O G H B C P X K J J M Y
S L E A D E R R X K C H L W T
U Y T Z H C I Y L G W U Z Y I
O T M B V F G O W B P Q P F R
I I S J V E X E M P L A R Y G
C C H E V I S S I M B U S J E
A A I K R E T C A R A H C M T
N G D I L I G E N T R Y M C N
E A C I V K F D S R N R R Q I
T S E R D H O I I R M E I W Y
```

Character	Instruction	Prudent	Submissive
Diligent	Integrity	Reverent	Tactful
Exemplary	Leader	Sagacity	Tenacious

LESSON 6

Topic: Setting Your Priorities by Discovering PURPOSE
(Based upon Jeremiah 29:11, NIV)

Opening Prayer

Keep it real and talk to God straight from your heart. Don't pretend or worry about who is looking at you. Remember, this is your relationship with God and no one else's.

Setting Your Priorities by Discovering Purpose

Your being able to discover your purpose is a simple yet difficult concept to grasp. Has anyone ever asked you what your purpose in life is and you really did not know how to answer that question? Many people have been there. Although most adults wish that our discovering our purpose was as simple as choosing an outfit every day, in most cases, it is a really complex issue. It is complex because purpose is about discovering what God specifically created you to do while on this Earth. It goes deeper than your possessing that talent of singing or dancing that you may have (although your talent may definitely go hand in hand with your purpose).

The key is to remember that your true purpose in life is not all about you—it is about your giving God the glory in what you do. It is about inspiring others and drawing them closer to Christ.

In order to set priorities, as people of Christ, we need to know where we are going. We need to know our purpose. Our knowing our purpose gives us the roadmap we need for our lives. I have not always known where I was going in my own life. I often ignored the roadmap that God had given me and decided to go my own way. Bad move. I am an example of someone who has truly struggled with purpose. At times, I felt like I was losing my mind. I am sure that some of us may be experiencing the same battles with purpose. My personal battle was directly connected to my self-esteem; I never believed that I had the right talents and abilities, or even the physical appearance to do what God had purposed for me to do. I often looked at some of my friends and believed that they were the ones with the talent. That was the worst thing I could have done. No one should ever compare himself or herself with another, because our purposes in life are different. God has a different plan for each of us, and when we compare, we are kind of telling God that we are not grateful for what He has for us. It is because of my lack of trust in God, my self-esteem issues, and my comparing my life to others' that I eventually gave up on my purpose. I just literally gave up. I chose (what I thought) was the "safe" route—a route that was comfortable and traditional. But anything outside of the will of God is never really safe. That route actually ended up being the miserable route; it was pure misery for me outside of God's will. I know from experience that, no matter how good a situation appears to be to others, or how much money one is making, he or she will never feel truly satisfied until he or she is in God's will. After years of fighting God's call, I had to finally surrender. Yielding to God's call is the best decision that I have ever made.

So my question to you is this: Do you know what your purpose is? Even if you say no, the truth is that you probably have been given a glimpse of an idea. It is already within you. What is that thing that you would do every day—if you did not have to worry about money or what people thought about you? What are your natural gifts and/or talents? What is "the voice" inside of you saying? What are the visions that you have for your life? Answering questions like these will help you get on track to discovering your purpose.

It is important to remember that your finding your purpose is (more often than not) a process. It is a process of discovering God. It is a process of discovering yourself. More importantly, it is about your learning to trust God and yourself. If you never trust and believe that God has a plan and purpose for you—and you do not trust yourself enough to trust God—then you will never go after what God has for you. You are going to have to really listen to yourself and God in order to hear what is inside your heart. You need to be honest with yourself and honest with God. If you do your part, then God will do the rest.

All in all, you must know that God has a purpose for your life. Do not let people's disapproval (even family and friends) or your own self-doubt keep you from what God has for you. Do your best to set the priority to find out your purpose and work toward it. Do not ever just settle for anything—because doing so will lead to regret. Regret then leads to misery. That is not the life that God wants for you. God has called you to do more and be more. Yes, there will be challenges. Yes, there will be rough times. Yes, you will have doubts. No, it will not be easy. Despite it all, just keep pushing along. Whatever God has purposed for you, God has already equipped you to do. Answer God's call for your life, no matter what it is. That will be the best call you will ever take. Then you will set your priorities on the things that God has for your life.

Break It Up!

Simon Says... Really!

Take one cup of crushed ice. Next, use the fork, spoon, or knife that you have been given to try to eat the crushed ice out of the cup. Does it work? Why or why not? Which instrument works better? Today's lesson is about discovering your calling or purpose. When God created you, He already had a calling or purpose for your life. Your calling is only for you and not for anyone else. It cannot be shared. Hopefully, you have noticed that the spoon may have been the best selection for eating the ice. The spoon met the purpose specifically of gathering up the crushed ice better because it is uniquely made to scoop and bring together liquids and solids. Similar to the spoon, you are uniquely made for your calling and purpose by God to perform those tasks that have been chosen for you to fulfill.

 You can listen to music while you complete this lesson.

Trending: #discoveryourpurpose

Essential Question

Do you know what your purpose is?

Purpose

 What's in a name? Use an Internet search engine to look up popular boy and girl names for newborns. When we are born, what we are named is important because names serve to identify who we are in the world. Names have meaning. See if you can find the meaning of your name or a name that is similar and relate the meaning of your name to the purpose of your life.

50 4-R.E.A.L.: Real Talk for Middle and High School Youth

Lesson Overview

God has called you to do more and be more. Yes, there will be challenges. Yes, there will be rough times. Yes, you will have doubts. No, it will not be easy. Despite it all, just keep pushing along.

No matter what purpose God has for you, He has already equipped you to do it. Answer God's call for your life, no matter what it is. That will be the best call you will ever take. Then you need to set your priorities on the things that God has for your life.

> **Jeremiah 29:11 (NIV)**
> 11 "For I know the plans I have for you," declares the Lord, "plans to prosper you and not to harm you, plans to give you hope and a future."

TIP—Training in Progress

Please understand that just as God knows your name, so does the enemy. Be careful to guard your name and the reputation that comes with it. Persons' reputations can either help or destroy them with other people. Make sure that you do all that you can to live a godly life and make a godly name for yourself.

Here are some **TIP**s:
- Not everyone that knows your name has godly intentions. Be careful!
- God knows everything about you and has purpose for your life.
- Though it may feel like you are forgotten, God knows your name even in the worst of times.
- The Holy Spirit has been described as having a still, small voice. You may be called to a special calling or to perform a certain action when you least expect it to bless someone else.
- It is important that we break away from all distractions like people, activities, cellphones, and television to become silent and still so that we can hear God's call.
- Always listen for God's voice.

Word Is Bond

 The denotation of a word means the literal meaning or definition from the dictionary. "Context" means how the word is used in a sentence, or vocabulary words that are used in a way that reveals their meaning.

Use an online dictionary to find out the following information about the word *priority*.

Find and write down the denotation of the word *priority*:

_____

_____

- What other words have the same meaning as *priority* (synonyms)?

Synonyms: _____

- What other words have the opposite meaning of *priority* (antonyms)?

Antonyms: _____

Context: What kind of priorities should be set in the order of importance in order to discover your purpose?

_____

_____

_____

When you are done writing, share your sentences with three people to see if their sentences match with your own.

Can you find words in other languages (like Greek, Latin, Spanish, Italian, or French) that mean the same as *priority*?

Reflection 3-2-1

Share your personal reflections on the lesson today with a selected partner that you have not yet had the chance to work with.

Find a partner with whom to discuss what you learned in today's lesson. Write down your answers, if needed. Your answers may not be duplicated.

- Name *three* points that you recall about today's lesson.
- What *two* aspects from the lesson did you learn that you didn't know before?
- Think of *one* question that you can ask your partner regarding today's lesson.

Circle Up...

True or False?
Read and mark the following statements with a **T** for true or **F** for false. If it is false, be ready to explain why.

_____ 1. We have to make God the number-one priority in our lives.
_____ 2. It is easy to discover our purpose.
_____ 3. Other people can also fulfill the purpose that God has designed for me.
_____ 4. We need direction from God in order to know our purpose.
_____ 5. Other friends have the talent and gifts to meet their purpose, but not me.
_____ 6. Finding your purpose is not going to be a process.
_____ 7. In order to find our purpose, we must discover ourselves.
_____ 8. We should let our family's and friends' opinions matter more than God's Word.
_____ 9. When we move in our purpose there will never be challenges.
_____ 10. God equips each of us to meet our purpose.
_____ 11. We do not have to answer God's call in order to have our purpose.

Closing Prayer

Come together to offer a group prayer to God. Don't forget that He knows your future. If you have any concerns that need to be addressed in prayer—such as scholarship applications, college applications, an ill family member, passing any tests, understanding your school subjects, and so forth—this is the time to pray for yourself and for each other. Discover your purpose!

Inter-Action! Worksheet Activity

What are your priorities when it comes to discovering your purpose? One of the ways of discovering your purpose is by looking at your name. But what about other aspects like the types of relationships in your life? What about other actions? Below, the word *priority* appears as an acrostic. Use each letter to describe an action that you must do in order to start discovering your purpose. For example, "P" could stand for "prayer." Once done, be ready to share with your classmates.

P _____

R _____

I _____

O _____

R _____

I _____

T _____

Y _____

LESSON 7

Topic: Celebrate Your Uniqueness: You Are More Important than You Realize
(Based upon Romans 2:11; Ephesians 4:11; Jeremiah 29:11, NIV)

Opening Prayer

Keep it real and talk to God straight from your heart. Don't pretend or worry about who is looking at you. Remember, this is your relationship with God and no one else's.

CELEBRATE YOUR UNIQUENESS:
You Are More Important than You Realize

GOD CREATED ALL PEOPLE ON THIS EARTH AS EQUAL, BUT EACH OF US HAS BEEN GIVEN OUR VERY OWN DISTINCTIVE LOOK, FACIAL FEATURES, GIFTS, TALENTS, AND ABILITIES. Although we are different, God loves us all equally, far beyond our level of comprehension. God's love for us is so great that He gave His only Son, Jesus Christ, as a sin offering, because we were all born sinful—with imperfections—and so that we could live in perfect harmony with Him. Even though God's love for us is expressed plainly and clearly in the Bible (and we all share in that same love), there are times when we may experience, or witness others experience, being singled out or mistreated because of our/their differences.

God did not intend for everyone to be exactly alike. If that were the case, then God would have made us all the same. Even in the church, He said that He handed out different gifts to His people: some apostles, some prophets, some evangelists, and some teachers—so that they would all work together to equip one another in unity, and build up one another in the oneness of Christ (see Ephesians 4:11). If we applied this same principle and belief to our lives today, we would see that each of us has a place and a purpose (no matter how different we are), and all lives are equally important.

Romans 2:11 tells us that God does not show favoritism. No matter what our capabilities are in life, God wants us to use what He has given us—our gifts, talents, and uniqueness—to help one another. Not only does He want us to help each other, but He also wants us to pool our talents and resources together in order to build loving relationships and accomplish great things in the body of Christ. For example, if you think about a basketball team and how well the teammates function together, you will see that while not everybody shoots three-pointers well, there are some individuals who are good at making three-point shots; and while not everyone on the team has the height to be a strong forward or center, the team does consist of a few forwards and centers; some on the team will be good rebounders, while some are not so good. However, with each person using his/her greatest strengths and skills, they come together to make up a powerful and skillful team that will possibly be victorious in winning the game. When the team wins, everyone on the team is a winner—even the ones who sat on the bench and cheered on their team members during the game. That is how God planned for us to interact with each other—using our unique talents and abilities in unity for greatness.

Being your own unique person sometimes may cause you to be rejected or may cause you to be considered a social outcast from your peers. Even in times when you are just standing up for what is right, you may be ridiculed. Not being accepted for whatever reason may cause you to have low self-esteem or cause you to go into a state of depression. During such difficult times in your teenage life, it may seem hard for you to find someone to talk to about your situation—for fear that you will be misunderstood or rejected.

Celebrating your uniqueness is a choice that you can make, even when other people have pointed out your differences in a negative way. For instance, if another person tells you that your hair is too curly or not curly enough, but deep down inside you like the way you wear your hair, then choose to be okay with it. On the other hand, if you yourself do not like your hair and you find a better style that you like then go for it. But, do not change your look just to please others—do it for yourself. Or, if you love to read books and you spend a lot of time doing so (instead of hanging out with the crowd), do not worry about what anybody else thinks of you—just be yourself, and do not be afraid of sharing it with others. You will be surprised at the fact that there may be others who have the same interests as you do. Who knows, you could be the one who starts a book club in your school!

Everyone needs encouragement and support, which helps you grow, gain courage, and reach your potential. Consider encouraging someone else who may be going through a difficult time in trying to fit in, or someone who may have a tough decision to make. Pray with the individual in faith—letting him or her know that God will lead him or her in the right direction, as long as he or she gives his or her thoughts to Him in faith. Then you will be surprised at how you played an important role in building up someone else's life, which in turn will encourage you to know that you, too, belong and your life is just as important. Philippians 2:4 reads, "Let each of you look out not only for his own interests, but also for the interests of others" (NKJV). Teens, you need to know that you are important, regardless of your gender, race, ethnicity, or any other difference you may have.

These are things to remember when feeling isolated or rejected:

You are never alone. No matter how alone or different you may feel, talk to someone like a teacher, a spiritual mentor, or friend, telling him or her about yourself and how you feel; or you can create a blog—opening up discussions on subjects that you are dealing with. You will find that there are many more teens just like you, so many more than you realize with whom you can connect.

Talk to God about everything. Philippians 4:6-7 reads, "Do not be anxious about anything, but in everything, by prayer and petition, with thanksgiving, present your requests to God. And the peace of God, which transcends all understanding, will guard your hearts and your minds in Christ Jesus."

Celebrate your uniqueness. God loves you just the way you are. He made you that way and gave you certain things that others do not have. It is when you accept that love from God that you are able to love yourself and share your uniqueness to help others.

You were created with a purpose. Jeremiah 29:11 reads, "'For I know the plans I have for you,' declares the Lord, 'plans to prosper you and not to harm you, plans to give you hope and a future.'"

Meditate on positive things. Philippians 4:8 reads, "Finally, brothers and sisters, whatever is true, whatever is noble, whatever is right, whatever is pure, whatever is lovely, whatever is admirable—if anything is excellent or praiseworthy—think about such things."

Be careful about comparing yourself to others. When you are competing with other people as a way of gaining acceptance or fitting in, this may lead you to failure or rejection.

Break It Up!

Take one compact mirror and open it up! Look at your reflection. Take time to look at your features—nose, ears, mouth, and all—and be ready to discuss the essential question below.

 You can listen to music while you complete this lesson.

Trending: #Iamunique

Essential Question

What makes YOU unique?

Purpose

 Self-esteem. So many teens, and even adults, have no self-esteem when it comes to loving and accepting how God has made them. God loves us all so deeply that we could never fully understand it. God has made each of us unique because we are the only ones designed to fulfill our individual purpose on Earth. Choose today to love who you are and *whose* you are. You belong to God!

Lesson Overview

God did not intend for everyone to be exactly alike. If that were the case, then God would have made us all the same. Even in the church, He said that He handed out different gifts to His people—some apostles, some prophets, some evangelists, and some teachers—so that they would all work together to equip one another in unity, and build up one another in the oneness of Christ (see Ephesians 4:11).

Each of us has a place and a purpose (no matter how different we are), and all lives are equally important.

> **Romans 2:11 (NIV)**
> 11 For God does not show favoritism.
>
> .....
>
> **Ephesians 4:11 (NIV)**
> 11 So Christ himself gave the apostles, the prophets, the evangelists, the pastors and teachers.
>
> .....
>
> **Jeremiah 29:11 (NIV)**
> 11 "For I know the plans I have for you," declares the Lord, "plans to prosper you and not to harm you, plans to give you hope and a future."

TIP—Training in Progress

You are distinct. There is no one on this Earth like you. No one has the same set of fingerprints. Even identical twins have their own unique set of fingerprints. God is that purposeful in how He created you so that you can reach your purpose.

Here are some **TIP**s:

- You were created with a purpose that was made just for you.
- Comparing yourself to other people is like saying that God doesn't know what He is doing.
- YOU ARE TO BE LOVED, ACCEPTED, AND CELEBRATED.
- If anyone in your life cannot love, accept, or celebrate you and your uniqueness, then separate yourself from them. They should be lifting you up, not bringing you down.

Word Is Bond

 The denotation of a word means the literal meaning or definition from the dictionary. "Context" means how the word is used in a sentence, or vocabulary words that are used in a way that reveals their meaning.

Use an online dictionary to find out the following information about the word *unique*.

Find and write down the denotation of the word *unique*:

_____

_____

- What other words have the same meaning as *unique* (synonyms)?

Synonyms: _____

- What other words have the opposite meaning of *unique* (antonyms)?

Antonyms: _____

Context: Now, see if you can use the word *unique* and a synonym and an antonym of it in sentences.

_____

_____

_____

When you are done writing, share your sentences with three people to see if their sentences match with your own.

Can you find words in other languages (like Greek, Latin, Spanish, Italian, or French) that mean the same as *unique*?

Reflection 3-2-1

Share your personal reflections on the lesson today with a selected partner that you have not yet had the chance to work with.

Find a partner with whom to discuss what you learned in today's lesson. Write down your answers, if needed. Your answers may not be duplicated.

- Name *three* points that you recall about today's lesson.
- What *two* aspects from the lesson did you learn that you didn't know before?
- Think of *one* question that you can ask your partner regarding today's lesson.

Circle Up...

Pay It Forward
As you join in the circle, be prepared to share one unique aspect about yourself. Then pay it forward by complimenting a unique aspect about someone else in the circle.

Closing Prayer

Come together to offer a group prayer to God. Don't forget that He knows your future. If you have any concerns that need to be addressed in prayer—such as scholarship applications, college applications, an ill family member, passing any tests, understanding your school subjects, and so forth—this is the time to pray for yourself and for each other. There is a call on your life to be a living example of God's Word.

Inter-Action! Worksheet Activity

What Are Your Strengths?

Please listen for the instructions from your teacher. Once you understand these instructions, type the link below into your browser and create an account. Take this survey to find out what some of your character strengths are, as we are celebrating your uniqueness and distinction! This is a free survey and should take only fifteen minutes to complete. When you are done with the survey, share what your character strengths are with each other.

(The VIA Institute on Character)
https://www.viacharacter.org/survey/account/register

LESSON 8

Topic: Get Your Shine On!
(Based upon John 9:5; Matthew 5:14-16, NIV)

Opening Prayer

Keep it real and talk to God straight from your heart. Don't pretend or worry about who is looking at you. Remember, this is your relationship with God and no one else's.

GET YOUR SHINE ON!

The 2012 Olympics gave all of us the opportunity to see athletes from all over the world—mostly younger than thirty years of age—display their unique physical and intellectual gifts on the world stage. From the most decorated Olympian of all time (Michael Phelps) to the unbelievably talented Gabby Douglas and Missy Franklin, to the "lightning bolt" (the world's fastest man—Usain Bolt), to those unstoppable sisters from California, Venus and Serena Williams, we have watched these athletes compete, cry, struggle, and overcome obstacles in order to represent their families, schools, communities, and churches, and the United States in ways that make us all proud. What they achieved in the 2012 Olympics will forever be etched into our hearts and minds and the history books. They unapologetically shined brightly on the biggest stage in the world. Although we may not have the same physical abilities as some of these great athletes, we still have been given direct instructions from Jesus to shine just as brightly as anyone else. And we are to do so, not to win a gold, silver, or bronze medal, but to show the world that Jesus is indeed real. Just like those Olympians, we possess the ability to be bright lights in a world that is in need of the powerful, life-giving light that comes from the God we serve. In the book of Matthew, Jesus has three objectives: to *preach*, *teach*, and *heal*.

When we come to this passage of Scripture, Jesus is teaching the famous Beatitudes—where He is empowering the people who are present by giving them a word of hope and help regarding God's divine order. By the time we reach the thirteenth verse, Jesus changes His tone from one of declaring blessings on the poor, meek, and merciful, to one of making some declarations about our identity as God's people. Initially, Jesus said that we are the "salt of the earth." Among its many uses, salt is used to preserve, add flavor to, and even purify things. By calling us salt, Jesus is declaring that we possess the ability to change the substance of or add flavor to something (like those greens or blackeyed peas that needed a little life), or actually to help preserve something that is already alive but is in need of sustained help. So in calling us salt, Jesus is clearly saying that we are a valuable and extremely useful resource on Earth. However, He is not finished—because Jesus moved from calling us salt (in verse 13) to then saying that we are "the lights of the world" (verse 14). Wow . . . what an honor to be called lights by Jesus! It is an honor because that is the same way Jesus referred to Himself in John 9:5; He said, **"As long as I am in the** world, I am the light of the world" (NKJV). But He did not stop there; He began to actually give us permission—better yet, a mandate—to *get our shine on*!

We are always being told to be humble—not to be flashy or to look for the spotlight. As a result, many of us will sit in the back of the classroom, never speak up when we see something wrong, not raise our hands when we know the answer, never make a new friend, or never try out for the football team, chess club, cheerleading squad, or basketball or tennis team. Or we may feel like because we are not as popular as this person or that person then we cannot be student government or class president. Well, in these verses, Jesus was telling those who were present then (and us who read and follow God's Word now) that we actually have a responsibility to shine for the Savior. We live in a world that is obsessed with "bling" and is always telling us to shine; we may spend our money on the shiniest 24- or 26-inch rims (and rent them if we cannot afford to buy them)—just so we can shine, or so we can "stunt" like we really got money (when we actually do not). Years ago, hip-hop mogul P. Diddy and Mase even wore shiny suits to promote a new era of bling-bling within hip-hop. That is a form of shining more for personal glory and being noticed by everybody for what you have than for letting the person you are come forth.

However, Jesus is telling us to shine, represent, or "put on" in a way that involves us but is not about us. So, to make sure that we will not get confused with shining for self over the Savior, Jesus laid out some quick instructions concerning how we are to shine. He says, **"A city on a hill cannot be hidden. Neither do people light a lamp and put it under a bowl. Instead they put it on its stand, and it gives light to everyone in the house"** (Matthew 5:14b-15, NIV). One thing Jesus is saying is that you are not to hide or be ashamed of who you are. You might not come from a great neighborhood, your school may be deemed sub-par, and you may not look like this person or that person, but you are still a child of God—and that is nothing to hide. Also, shining for the Savior means that we take responsibility to help others and we make sure that we do not hog all the light; instead, we are to put the light on a stand or lift it up, so that everybody in the house can see the God of our salvation. We are supposed to put our light in a position so that other people can see their way a little bit clearer or find their way out of a situation, because they used our light as a guide. This simply means that when we have been given an opportunity, we do what we can to make sure that we are not the only ones who will benefit. Where would we be if people only kept the light in their house? If Dr. King or Mary McLeod Bethune had kept their lights hidden, we would not have Bethune Cookman College and many of the civil liberties we enjoy right now.

Jesus is talking about our responsibility to the community, which includes our churches, schools, families, and local neighborhoods. After He addresses the communal, He moves to the personal: **"In the same way, let your light shine before others, that they may see your good deeds and praise your Father in heaven"** (Matthew 5:16, NIV). Right here, Jesus makes it clear that you have a duty—an obligation—to "Get Yo' Shine On!" In other words, you are to let your light shine . . . whatever that light is. Some of us shine in math; others shine in science or reading; for others, it is singing, preaching, public speaking, basketball, baseball, chess, tennis, soccer, playing an instrument, dancing, teaching, and so forth where they may shine. Whatever it is, Jesus is saying that we need not be afraid or ashamed, because what we have needs to be seen—not just so people will know our names, but so that people will know and glorify *His* name. When we shine with the gifts that God has given us, we show others that Jesus really lives and that He lives in us; He is calling us to shine in the classroom, on the basketball/tennis court, and in our churches—for the good of our families, our communities, and our world. So do not delay—**get your shine on today!**

Break It Up!

Locate the flashlight or torch application on your cellphones and turn it on. Your teacher will darken the room. What do you notice when your lights are on in the darkened room? Does the darkness stay or go? Be prepared for a class discussion on becoming shiners for Jesus Christ!

 You can listen to music while you complete this lesson.

Trending: #Shiner

Essential Question

Are you afraid to shine?

Purpose

 Be a shiner! In the present society, there is more of a glorification of mediocrity, hypocrisy, and absurdity in schools, music, movies, and so forth. God needs you to bring light to a world of darkness. Don't be afraid to shine although other people you may know choose to revel in foolish behavior. Dare to be different. That's what Jesus Christ wants us to be—lights in a world of darkness.

Lesson Overview

When we shine with the gifts that God has given us, we show others that Jesus really lives and that He lives in us. He is calling us to shine in the classroom, on the basketball/tennis court, and in our churches—for the good of our families, our communities, and our world.

So do not delay—get your shine on today!

John 9:5 (NIV)
5 "While I am in the world, I am the light of the world."

·····

Matthew 5:14-16 (NIV)
14 "You are the light of the world. A town built on a hill cannot be hidden. 15 Neither do people light a lamp and put it under a bowl. Instead they put it on its stand, and it gives light to everyone in the house. 16 In the same way, let your light shine before others, that they may see your good deeds and glorify your Father in heaven."

TIP—Training in Progress

Here are some **TIP**s:

- Just as you cannot extinguish a light by hiding it under a bowl, do not extinguish your light either.

- Jesus is light!

- Don't apologize to anyone because you are capable and unique. This is how God made you.

- When you are not afraid to shine, others will become encouraged to shine their lights, too.

- Your light is put on the inside of you to help other people.

- Those that hide their lights eventually will "catch fire" if they won't follow God's Word and shine for Him.

Word Is Bond

 The denotation of a word means the literal meaning or definition from the dictionary. "Context" means how the word is used in a sentence, or vocabulary words that are used in a way that reveals their meaning.

Use an online dictionary to find out the following information about the word *illuminate*.

Find and write down the denotation of the word *illuminate*:

_____

_____

- What other words have the same meaning as *illuminate* (synonyms)?

Synonyms: _____

- What other words have the opposite meaning of *illuminate* (antonyms)?

Antonyms: _____

Context: Now, see if you can use the word *illuminate* and a synonym and an antonym of it in sentences.

_____

_____

_____

When you are done writing, share your sentences with three people to see if their sentences match with your own.

Can you find words in other languages (like Greek, Latin, Spanish, Italian, or French) that mean the same as *illuminate*?

Reflection 3-2-1

Share your personal reflections on the lesson today with a selected partner that you have not yet had the chance to work with.

Find a partner with whom to discuss what you learned in today's lesson. Write down your answers, if needed. Your answers may not be duplicated.

- Name *three* points that you recall about today's lesson.
- What *two* aspects from the lesson did you learn that you didn't know before?
- Think of *one* question that you can ask your partner regarding today's lesson.

Circle Up…

One-word Whiparound
Stand together in the circle. Your teacher is going to make a statement, and you must guess which one word makes it unique. Quickly respond with your one-word answer when your teacher gives you a prompt about today's lesson. *Example:* "The weather is hot outside today." *Student response:* "Hot."

Listen for the prompts from your teacher and get ready to give those one-word responses.

Closing Prayer

Come together to offer a group prayer to God. Don't forget that He knows your future. If you have any concerns that need to be addressed in prayer—such as scholarship applications, college applications, an ill family member, passing any tests, understanding your school subjects, and so forth—this is the time to pray for yourself and for each other. There is a call on your life to be a living example of God's Word.

Inter-Action! Worksheet Activity

SKIT
Create Your Own Talk Show

The purpose of talk shows is to inform, educate, or entertain. They are comprised of a host who asks questions to create dialogue with guests or audience members.

The purpose of this talk-show skit is to celebrate the purpose and uniqueness of all of you. You may work as a class or have separate groups of four, depending on the class size. The talk-show host must come up with eight questions based upon the eight topics that were covered in this unit. The guests are the students in the groups. No celebrity impersonations or pretend characters are permitted. Remember, this is about celebrating you and your getting your moment to shine.

For example, one host question could be, "How do you keep your hope strong with so much negativity in today's society?"

Have fun!
Be creative!
Be a shiner!

Introduction to Group Facilitator's Tips
(Relevant, Engaging, and Alive Lessons)

These student-led lessons are designed to facilitate real conversations for our youth of today and tomorrow. Your role, as teacher, is to be a compassionate and understanding facilitator. No judgment allowed. Create the environment needed to bring about real discussion of today's obstacles of faith. Use this as a reference page for understanding the icons and the sections. Thank you for your role as facilitator and making the choice to invest in the lives of youth. Thank you for being 4REAL!

CONTENT GUIDE FOR THE LESSONS:

Opening Prayer: No scripted prayers here. Encourage the teens to speak from their own minds and hearts. Remind them that their prayers do not have to sound ceremonious. Teens have to get used to having authentic communication with God. It is all right to model a prayer for the youth to see and hear.

Article: After the opening prayer there is an article that coincides with the topic of the lesson. Please read it as a class.

Break It Up!: This section provides an icebreaker to warm up the students before going into the lesson. Think of brief but welcoming activities to help the teens begin interaction.

The students are encouraged to listen to music as they complete the lesson.

Trending: Encourage the teens to put positive phrases on social-media sites.

Essential Question: This area will have a starter question or activity that is the seed for the day's lesson. This is to lead to discussion to answer the essential question and begin the interaction.

Purpose: This is the time of recognizing their purpose and understanding that God has plans for them to fulfill that are for them only. They will look at the essential question as it relates to their direction. Students can use the lined writing pages in their books.

Lesson Overview: There will always be a small paragraph from the article that relates to the lesson. Encourage students to read and underline any words that are unfamiliar each time they read in this area. Summarize key points from the lesson. Point out its connection (God's advice) to the Bible passage.

Lesson Scripture Passage: This is the lesson Scripture passage that relates to the lesson.

TIP (Training in Progress): This section provides godly advice for today's youth when their faith may be challenged. Also gain, social-media TIPs on how to interact responsibly and have an online presence, while balancing life. Cellphones can be used as a learning tool in the lessons if it doesn't cause distraction.

Word Is Bond: In this section, students interact with God's Word. Vocabulary words and other words are also explored to help build and explore unfamiliar vocabulary for greater understanding.

Reflection 3-2-1: This section gives students the chance to reflect on their lesson and subject matter and how they can make it relevant for their lives. Students will collaborate and discuss answers that are not duplicated.

Circle Up...: This section gives students an opportunity to further reflect on the lesson in pairs or groups.

Closing Prayer: Everyone comes together to agree in prayer regarding collective/individual issues that are trying their faith.

Inter-Action!: These are activities designed with youth in mind for critical thinking, discussion, and action among the teens to exercise their faith despite the obstacles. Worksheets are reproducible.

Group Facilitator's Tips: Lesson 1

TOPIC: Not without Hope: The Lives of Teens in the Age of the New Millennium and Beyond
(Based upon Romans 5:1-11, NIV)

Opening Prayer: Encourage youth to speak from their own minds and hearts. Let them know that it doesn't have to sound ceremonious or contain big words. Model a prayer for the teens to hear first. Then ask if they all want to pray in a circle, with each person saying a short prayer; or select one person to offer a collective prayer.

Article: Read the lesson's accompanying article as a class.

Break It Up!— *"Name Tent" Icebreaker:* The students will follow the directions for making their own name tents to introduce themselves to their classmates. These tents can remain throughout the duration of any future lessons for recall, arranging seats, and so forth. You will need crayons, markers, and paper—(colored construction paper, copy paper and so forth).

Materials Needed: construction paper (in various colors), crayons, markers, copy paper, pencils, Bibles

Since teens like to work with their cellphones and listen to music, check that they have entered an appropriate link. If there are some who do not have a phone or earbuds, play some music softly in class while they are working.

Trending: #notwithouthope

Essential Question: After the students solve the puzzle, strike up a discussion to see what they are thinking about this question. Lead them to discuss this question and their answers. When people compare their lives to other people's, they are putting themselves at risk of living without hope. This is the puzzle's answer: ***Are you rejecting God's Word when you compare your life to someone else's?***

Purpose: After having the teens discuss their ideas, have them write them down as they are discovering that they have a unique, individual purpose that God has created them to accomplish on Earth that no one else can do. If they need more writing space, keep some filler paper around for extra writing.

Lesson Overview: Give an overview of the lesson. Read one paragraph aloud to model for them how to speak clearly and loud enough while reading. Then explain that they have the choice to do "relay reading" by reading a paragraph and then selecting a classmate to read, or to choose a reading partner and read to each other. Encourage the students to underline any words or concepts that may be unfamiliar to them. They can number each paragraph for quick reference in case they need to refer to it for an answer or as textual evidence. Summarize key points from the lesson. Point out its connection (God's advice) to the Bible passage.

Lesson Scripture Passage: Read the lesson Scripture passage that relates to the lesson.

TIP (Training in Progress): When many youth are away from home or are otherwise not under a watchful eye, sometimes integrity can be questioned or faith forgotten because they forget about God's Word. This could be while attending school, going to social events, or moving away from home after graduation. Remember that God's Word is not a suggestion; it is a way of life in everything that you do and say.

Word Is Bond: Perseverance is one of the qualities needed to live with hope. God's Word strengthens and fortifies His people when they are faced with obstacles. Have the students read the Scripture on perseverance. This area would be for vocabulary that would consist of not only the word but also where to find and look it up on their phone. Students will also discover how it is pronounced, the synonyms and antonyms of the word, and its origin.

When they are done writing, have them share their sentences with three classmates.

Reflection 3-2-1: This section gives students the chance to reflect on their lesson and subject matter and how they can make it relevant for their lives. If students need to write down this activity, give them some lined paper. Each student must have something different, if at all possible.

Circle Up…: After sharing their reflections about today's lesson with their partner, make a circle so each person can share one reflection and explain what they learned from the lesson.

Closing Prayer: This is also the time for those who may want collective prayer for a situation. Offer a prayer of thanks to God for today's lesson. Encourage the students to remember to "keep it real" with God, because He has real answers for real problems of today's world.

Inter-Action!: This is an activity used in classrooms to promote creative and critical thinking through the use of questioning. If you have never participated in or directed a Socratic seminar before, please investigate this information on the Internet. This activity can be used for almost any subject matter that is appropriate for public discussion. Type this link into your browser to learn more: https://www.youtube.com/watch?v=_CPLu3qCbSU

Group Facilitator's Tips: Lesson 2

TOPIC: Hope: The Expectation of Something Good
(Based upon Jeremiah 29, NIV)

 **Opening Prayer:** Encourage group members to speak from their own minds and hearts. Model a prayer for the teens to hear first. Then ask if they all want to pray in a circle, with each person saying a short prayer; or select one person to offer a collective prayer.

Article: Read the lesson's accompanying article as a class.

Break It Up!—*"Name Tent" Icebreaker:* In the previous lesson, the students made their own name tents to introduce themselves to their classmates. This icebreaker is for recalling names and what they learned about each other.

Materials Needed: crayons, markers, paper (colored construction paper, copy paper, and so forth)—just in case there is a new student who did not attend the previous lesson. Also, bring some treats or an inexpensive prize as a reward for those that recite the most names. Be creative!

 Play some music softly in class while the students are working.

Trending: #greatexpectations

Essential Question: Allow the students time to work the puzzle. Once the answer has been solved by the students, have them discuss what this means and challenge them to find the Bible verse related to the question (Jeremiah 32:27). Ask them how this relates to the topic of the lesson today. The answer for the puzzle is as follows: *"Is there anything too hard for God?"*

 **Purpose:** Allow the students time to write a six-sentence paragraph on what their purpose is by answering the essential question of today's lesson.

Lesson Overview: Give an overview of the lesson. Read one paragraph aloud to model for them how to speak clearly and loud enough while reading. Then explain that they have the choice to do "relay reading" by reading a paragraph and then selecting a classmate to read, or to choose a reading partner and read to each other. Encourage the students to underline any words or concepts that may be unfamiliar to them. They can number each paragraph for quick reference in case they need to refer to it for an answer or as textual evidence.

Lesson Scripture Passage: Read the lesson Scripture passage that relates to the lesson.

TIP (Training in Progress): *Discussion:* The Age of the New Millennium is not only a world of heavy distractions, but it can leave you with very little hope of anything getting better. Where do you place your hope? Do you hope in humans? Money? Education? Degrees? Social connections? Friends? Family? Can any of these areas bring us closer to God? Or do they drive us farther away from Him? Think about the last time you became discouraged in someone or something. What did you do to regain your hope?

Word Is Bond: Perseverance is one of the qualities needed to live with hope. God's Word strengthens and fortifies His people when they meet obstacles. Have the students read the Scripture on perseverance. This area would be for a vocabulary exercise that would consist not only of the word but also where to find and look it up on their phone. Students will also discover how it also pronounced, the synonyms and antonyms of the word, and its origin.

Reflection 3-2-1: This section gives students the chance to reflect on their lesson and subject matter and how they can make it relevant for their lives. If students need to write down this activity, give them some lined paper. Each student must have different responses, if at all possible.

Circle Up...: After forming a circle with their classmates, let the students take turns expressing one expectation of hope that they have of God's power in their lives.

Closing Prayer: This is also the time for those who may want collective prayer for a situation.

Inter-Action!: This is an activity for creating a vision board that will be used as a class collage. Every student should create their own individual vision board. First, help the students decide if they want to create a group vision board for their class and how they want to grow in the Word of God together. Or they can create individual vision boards about their own lives. Do they want to envision a certain period of time, like ten or twenty years into the future? Or a lifelong vision?

Group Facilitator's Tips: Lesson 3

TOPIC: Don't Lose Hope
(Based upon the Book of Habakkuk, NIV)

This lesson should be student-led with active student participation, and the teacher should serve as a facilitator only of the lesson.

 **Opening Prayer:** Encourage the students to speak from their own minds and hearts. Model a prayer for the teens to hear first. Then ask if they all want to pray in a circle, with each person saying a short prayer; or select one person to offer a collective prayer.

Article: Read the lesson's accompanying article as a class.

Break It Up!—*Materials Needed:* crayons, markers, paper (colored construction paper, copy paper, and so forth)

Directions: Pass out paper to the students and then on a sheet of paper, have them create an acrostic of the word HOPE. When they have finished, encourage them to share their acrostics with each other.

 Play some music softly in class while the students are working.

Trending: #restorationhope

Essential Question: Have the students answer the following question: ***What do you know or want to know or learn about the restoration of hope?***

 **Purpose:** Allow the students to select their own partner at your discretion to work on filling in the "K" and "W" of the chart. In the "K" section, they are to list any prior information that they already know about the topic of today's lesson. In the "W" section, they are to list any questions, clarifying issues, and so forth.

Lesson Overview: Give an overview of the lesson. Read one paragraph aloud to model for them how to speak clearly and loud enough while reading. Then explain that they have the choice to do "relay reading" by reading a paragraph and then selecting a classmate to read, or to choose a reading partner and read to each other. Encourage the students to underline any words or concepts that may be unfamiliar to them. They can number each paragraph for quick reference in case they need to refer to it for an answer or as textual evidence. Summarize key points from the lesson. Point out its connection (God's advice) to the Bible passage.

Lesson Scripture Passage: Read the lesson Scripture passage that relates to the lesson.

TIP (Training in Progress): *Discussion:* If there is restoration of hope, that means at one point hope was lost or discouraged. Think about the last time you became discouraged in someone or something. What did you do to regain your hope? How did you restore your hope in someone else who may have lost it due to the death of a loved one, the loss of a job, divorce, and so forth?

Word Is Bond: God's Word strengthens and fortifies His people when they are faced with obstacles. Have the students read the Scripture related to the word *restore*. This area would be for a vocabulary exercise that would consist not only of the word but also where to find and look it up on their phone. Students will also discover how it is pronounced, the synonyms and antonyms of the word, and its origin.

Reflection 3-2-1: This section gives students the chance to reflect on their lesson and subject matter and how they can make it relevant for their lives. If students need to write down this activity, give them some lined paper. Each student must have different responses, if at all possible.

As a class discuss the "K" and "W" sections of the listed chart, but don't discuss the "L" section yet!.

Circle Up…: Task the students with completing the "L" column of the KWL chart with their partners.

Have the students form a circle with their classmates then take turns expressing one expectation of hope that they have of God's power in their lives.

Closing Prayer: This is also the time for those who may want collective prayer for a situation.

Inter-Action!: Here is an opportunity for the class to come up with community projects. Note that one way that a person can regain hope is to take the time to serve others and not dwell on the problem. God is so much bigger than our problems.

Group Facilitator's Tips: Lesson 4

TOPIC: Hush! Somebody Is Calling Your Name!
(Based upon Isaiah 43:1; Jeremiah 1:5, NIV)

Material Needed: index cards, pens/pencils, copy paper

Opening Prayer: Encourage group members to speak from their own minds and hearts. Model a prayer for the teens to hear first. Then ask if they all want to pray in a circle, with each person saying a short prayer; or select one person to offer a collective prayer.

Article: Read the lesson's accompanying article as a class.

Break It Up! Pass out an index card to each student.

Today's lesson title is borrowed from a popular Negro spiritual. Remind the students that God loves us so much that He knows our names and doesn't forget who we are as individuals. He has a calling for each of our lives.

Many students may not recognize or know about Negro spirituals, where they come from, and their purpose. There are stereotypes that may muddle their understanding about this art form. Try to conduct some research beforehand on Negro spirituals in order to help them learn more about them.

Read and listen to the information found at this link to find out more information: https://www.loc.gov/item/ihas.200197495/.

Play some music softly in class while the students are working.

Trending: #Godknowsmyname

Essential Question: Allow the students to answer the following question: ***Do you know what to do when God calls your name?***

Purpose: After having the teens discuss their ideas, have them write them down as they are discovering that they have a unique, individual purpose that God has created them to accomplish on Earth that no one else can do. If they need more writing space, keep some paper around for extra writing.

4-R.E.A.L.: Real Talk for Middle and High School Youth

Lesson Overview: Give an overview of the lesson. Read one paragraph aloud to model for them how to speak clearly and loud enough while reading. Then explain that they have the choice to do "relay reading" by reading a paragraph and then selecting a classmate to read, or to choose a reading partner and read to each other. Encourage the students to underline any words or concepts that may be unfamiliar to them. They can number each paragraph for quick reference in case they need to refer to it for an answer or as textual evidence. Summarize key points from the lesson. Point out its connection (God's advice) to the Bible passage.

Lesson Scripture Passage: Read the lesson Scripture passage that relates to the lesson.

TIP (Training in Progress)—*Discussion:* Please understand that just as God knows your name, so does the enemy. Be careful of your name and the reputation that comes with it. Persons' reputations can either help or destroy them with other people. Make sure that you do all that you can to live a godly life and make a godly name for yourself.

Here are some more **TIP**s to add to the ones in the student lesson:
- Don't ignore the calling of God. When He calls, answer immediately through action.
- God knows everything about you and has purpose for your life.
- Your task is meant just for you to complete and no one else.
- Follow God's directions for the task(s) that you must complete.
- What are you passionate about?
- Exercise your talents. It could be music, writing, speaking, cooking, cleaning, etc.
- Sometimes, tasks will change.
- Always listen for God's call.

Word Is Bond: Explain to the students that an *epithet* is a brief, descriptive phrase that helps to characterize a particular person or object. Thousands of years ago, including the biblical times, epithets were used to describe a person, their reputation, and their bloodline.

Reflection 3-2-1: This section gives students the chance to reflect on their lesson and subject matter and how they can make it relevant for their lives. If students need to write down this activity, give them some lined paper. Each student must have different responses, if at all possible.

Circle Up…: This section gives students an opportunity to further reflect on the lesson in pairs or groups.

Closing Prayer: This is also the time for those who may want collective prayer for a situation.

Inter-Action!: *Create Your Own Epithet Collaborative Poster*

Materials Needed: crayons, markers, copy paper, construction paper, stencils, glitter glue, butcher paper

Pass out the materials to the students so they can complete the activity.

Group Facilitator's Tips: Lesson 5

TOPIC: What's Your Calling?
(Based upon Exodus 3-4, NIV)

 **Opening Prayer:** Encourage group members to speak from their own minds and hearts. Model a prayer for the teens to hear first. Then ask if they all want to pray in a circle, with each person saying a short prayer; or select one person to offer a collective prayer.

Article: Read the lesson's accompanying article as a class.

Break It Up!—*Simon Says…Really!* Answering God's call takes listening and following instructions that God gives to us in order to reach our purpose. The game "Simon Says" is a popular game that deals with hearing instructions and knowing how to respond properly. Select a volunteer to be Simon. Allow the students to play a few rounds of this game until there is a winner. Relate the game to hearing God's voice and following His instructions.

Materials Needed: an inexpensive prize for the winner

 Play some music softly in class while the students are working.

Trending: #Godiscallingyou

Essential Question: Begin a discussion to see what students are thinking about this question. Have them discuss this question and give their answers. Do they know what to do when God calls them for a task? Here is the question: ***Do you know what to do when God calls your name?***

 Purpose: Have the students write a six-sentence paragraph on what their purpose is by answering this essential question of today's lesson.

Lesson Overview: Give an overview of the lesson. Read one paragraph aloud to model for them how to speak clearly and loud enough while reading. Then explain that they have the choice to do "relay reading" by reading a paragraph and then selecting a classmate to read, or to choose a reading partner and read to each other. Encourage the students to underline any words or concepts that may be unfamiliar to them. They can number each paragraph for quick reference in case they need to refer to it for an answer or as textual evidence. Summarize key points from the lesson. Point out its connection (God's advice) to the Bible passage.

Lesson Scripture Passage: Read the lesson Scripture passage that relates to the lesson.

TIP (Training in Progress): Read over and discuss the TIPs provided in the student lesson.

Word Is Bond: Being passionate is one of the qualities needed to answer the call of God. God's call will help you recognize your purpose. This area would be for a vocabulary exercise that would consist not only of the word but also where to find and look it up on their phone. Students will also discover how it is pronounced, the synonyms and antonyms of the word, and its origin.

Reflection 3-2-1: This section gives students the chance to reflect on their lesson and subject matter and how they can make it relevant for their lives. If students need to write down this activity, give them some lined paper. Each student must have different responses, if at all possible.

Circle Up…: *Materials Needed:* large Post-it® notes

Each of the papers should bear one of the labels "Strongly Agree," "Agree," "Disagree," or "Strongly Disagree." Once they are labeled, post them in four different areas on the walls of the room. As the statements are read aloud, instruct the students to respond by standing by one of the statements. For example, if you say, "God called Moses to lead the Israelites," the students will not voice their response but will move quietly to one of the posted papers. After the students arrive there, select one of them to respond as to why he or she made that choice. Read the directions listed below and make sure that the students understand what they need to do.

Four Corners: *Statements to read aloud:*

1. We must seek God every day in His Word and our prayers.
2. If my parent has a call on his or her life, then the call on my life will be just like his/hers.
3. When God calls, He will give general instructions.
4. Answering God's call is easy.

 Closing Prayer: This is also the time for those who may want collective prayer for a situation.

 Inter-Action!: Allow the students to practice their spelling skills by finding vocabulary words in the word search. Like many people who are searching for their purpose, they are going to search in the puzzle, but if they trust God and answer His call they will realize their purpose in Him. After the students find the words, give them some time to look up the words and learn their definitions or meaning. This could be the time for more class discussion.

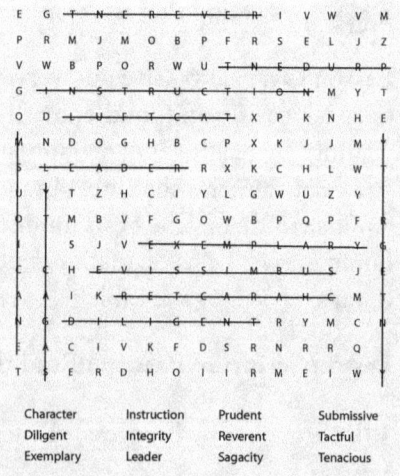

Character, Instruction, Prudent, Submissive
Diligent, Integrity, Reverent, Tactful
Exemplary, Leader, Sagacity, Tenacious

82   4-R.E.A.L.: Real Talk for Middle and High School Youth

Group Facilitator's Tips: Lesson 6

TOPIC: Setting Your Priorities by Discovering PURPOSE
(Based upon Jeremiah 29:11, NIV)

Opening Prayer: Encourage group members to speak from their own minds and hearts. Model a prayer for the teens to hear first. Then ask if they all want to pray in a circle, with each person saying a short prayer; or select one person to offer a collective prayer.

Article: Read the lesson's accompanying article as a class.

Break It Up!: In order to discover their own unique purpose, relate the game to hearing and obeying God's voice and finding one's purpose in life.

Materials Needed: plastic spoons and forks, bags of crushed ice, plastic cups, cooler

 Play some music softly in class while the students are working.

Trending: #discoveryourpurpose

Essential Question: Begin a discussion to see what students are thinking about this question. Have them discuss this question and give their answers: ***Do you know what your purpose is?***

Purpose: *Discussion:* What's in a name? Use an Internet search engine to look up popular boy and girl names for newborns. When we are born, what we are named is important because names serve to identify who we are in the world. Names have meaning. See if you can find the meaning of your name or a name that is similar and relate the meaning of your name to the purpose of your life.

Lesson Overview: Give an overview of the lesson. Read one paragraph aloud to model for them how to speak clearly and loud enough while reading. Then explain that they have the choice to do "relay reading" by reading a paragraph and then selecting a classmate to read, or to choose a reading partner and read to each other. Encourage the students to underline any words or concepts that may be unfamiliar to them. They can number each paragraph for quick reference in case they need to refer to it for an answer or as textual evidence. Summarize key points from the lesson. Point out its connection (God's advice) to the Bible passage.

TIP (Training in Progress): *Emphasize this:* Please understand that just as God knows your name, so does the enemy. Be careful to guard your name and the reputation that comes with it. Persons' reputations can either help or destroy them with other people. Make sure that you do all that you can to live a godly life and make a godly name for yourself.

Word Is Bond: This area would be for a vocabulary exercise that would consist not only of the word but also where to find and look it up on their phone. Students will also discover how it is pronounced, the synonyms and antonyms of the word, and its origin.

Reflection 3-2-1: This section gives students the chance to reflect on their lesson and subject matter and how they can make it relevant for their lives. If students need to write down this activity, give them some lined paper. Each student must have different responses, if at all possible.

Circle Up…: After students gather in a circle, have them complete the "True or False?" activity. During the review, have them discuss and defend their choice of responses—especially statements marked "false."

Answers:
1. **T**
2. **F**
3. **F**
4. **T**
5. **F**
6. **F**
7. **T**
8. **F**
9. **F**
10. **T**
11. **F**

Closing Prayer: This is also the time for those who may want collective prayer for a situation.

Inter-Action!: Ask, "What are your priorities when it comes to discovering your purpose? One of the ways of discovering your purpose is looking at your name, but what about other aspects like the types of relationships in your life? What about other actions? On the activity sheet, the word *priority* appears as an acrostic. Use each letter to describe an action that you must do in order to start discovering your purpose. For example, 'P' could stand for 'prayer.' Be ready to share your work with your classmates."

Group Facilitator's Tips: Lesson 7

TOPIC: Celebrate Your Uniqueness: You Are More Important than You Realize
(Based upon Romans 2:11; Ephesians 4:11; Jeremiah 29:11, NIV)

 **Opening Prayer:** Encourage group members to speak from their own minds and hearts. Model a prayer for the teens to hear first. Then ask if they all want to pray in a circle, with each person saying a short prayer; or select one person to offer a collective prayer.

Article: Read the lesson's accompanying article as a class.

Break It Up!: To help students discover their unique qualities, hand them a compact mirror. These are usually inexpensive and can be found in most area discount or "dollar" stores. Explain that God gives us not only unique physical characteristics but also characteristics on the inside that help us reach our purpose.

Materials Needed: compact or hand-held mirrors

 Play some music softly in class while they are working.

Trending: #Iamunique

Essential Question: Begin a discussion to see what students are thinking about this question. Have them discuss this question and give their answers: ***What makes YOU unique?***

 **Purpose:** Discuss self-esteem. ***Discussion:*** So many teens, and even adults, have no self-esteem when it comes to loving and accepting how God has made them. God loves us all so deeply that we could never fully understand it. God has made each of us unique because we are the only ones designed to fulfill our individual purpose on Earth. Choose today to love who you are and whose you are. You belong to God!

Lesson Overview: Give an overview of the lesson. Read one paragraph aloud to model for them how to speak clearly and loud enough while reading. Then explain that they have the choice to do "relay reading" by reading a paragraph and then selecting a classmate to read, or to choose a reading partner and read to each other. Encourage the students to underline any words or concepts that may be unfamiliar to them. They can number each paragraph for quick reference in case they need to refer to it for an answer or as textual evidence. Summarize key points from the lesson. Point out its connection (God's advice) to the Bible passage.

Lesson Scripture Passage: Read the lesson Scripture passage that relates to the lesson.

TIP (Training in Progress): *Discussion:* You are distinct. There is no one on this Earth like you. No one has the same set of fingerprints. Even identical twins have their own unique set of fingerprints. God is that purposeful in how He created you so that you can reach your purpose.

Word Is Bond: What does it mean to be unique? Allow the students time to complete this section. This area would be for a vocabulary exercise that would consist not only of the word but also where to find and look it up on their phone. Students will also discover how it is pronounced, the synonyms and antonyms of the word, and its origin.

Reflection 3-2-1: This section gives students the chance to reflect on their lesson and subject matter and how they can make it relevant for their lives. If students need to write down this activity, give them some lined paper. Each student must have different responses, if at all possible.

Circle Up…: *Pay It Forward:* Students need to realize that they should not only focus on their own uniqueness, but also compliment the uniqueness of others. In this activity, the students will affirm themselves and then see how their positive words can edify someone else. The student first shares a unique personal characteristic, then with the person standing to their left, they will recognize a unique outward or inward characteristic and pay that student a compliment (one that is appropriate, nice, and respectful). This should be done around the circle until everyone has had a turn.

Closing Prayer: This is also the time for those who may want collective prayer for a situation.

Inter-Action!: Please preview and use the following link to help your students discover their unique strengths: https://www.viacharacter.org/survey/account/register. A printed version of the survey is available at http://www.bethlehemschools.org/wp-content/uploads/VIA-Character-Strengths-Discussion-Survey.pdf.

Group Facilitator's Tips: Lesson 8

TOPIC: Get Your Shine On!
(Based upon John 9:5; Matthew 5:14-16, NIV)

 **Opening Prayer:** Encourage group members to speak from their own minds and hearts. Model a prayer for the teens to hear first. Then ask if they all want to pray in a circle, with each person saying a short prayer; or select one person to offer a collective prayer.

Article: Read the lesson's accompanying article as a class.

Break It Up:! Ask the students to locate the flashlight or torch application on their cellphones and turn them on. Turn off the lights in the room or darken the room so they can see the difference their lights shining in the dark makes. Ask them, "What do you notice when your lights are shining in the room? What happens to the darkness?" Then lead them in a discussion about what it means to shine their lights for Jesus and why it is important.

 Play some music softly in class while the students are working.

Trending: #Shiner

Essential Question: Begin a discussion to see what students are thinking about this question. Have them discuss this question and give their answers: ***Are you afraid to shine?***

 **Purpose: *Discuss:*** Be a shiner! In the present society, there is more of a glorification of mediocrity, hypocrisy, and absurdity in schools, music, movies, and so forth. God needs you to bring light to a world of darkness. Don't be afraid to shine although other people you may know choose to revel in foolish behavior. Dare to be different. That's what Jesus Christ wants us to be—lights in a world of darkness.

Lesson Overview: Give an overview of the lesson. Read one paragraph aloud to model for them how to speak clearly and loud enough while reading. Then explain that they have the choice to do "relay reading" by reading a paragraph and then selecting a classmate to read, or to choose a reading partner and read to each other. Encourage the students to underline any words or concepts that may be unfamiliar to them. They can number each paragraph for quick reference in case they need to refer to it for an answer or as textual evidence. Summarize key points from the lesson. Point out its connection (God's advice) to the Bible passage.

Lesson Scripture Passage: Read the lesson Scripture passage that relates to the lesson.

TIP (Training in Progress): Read over and discuss the TIPs provided in the student lesson.

Word Is Bond: What does it mean to illuminate? Allow the students time to complete this section. This area would be for a vocabulary exercise that would consist not only of the word but also where to find and look it up on their phone. Students will also discover how it is pronounced, the synonyms and antonyms of the word, and its origin.

Reflection 3-2-1: This section gives students the chance to reflect on their lesson and subject matter and how they can make it relevant for their lives. If students need to write down this activity, give them some lined paper. Each student must have different responses, if at all possible.

Circle Up…: *One-word Whiparound*

Activity found at *(http://www.theteachertoolkit.com/index.php/tool/whip-around)*

1. **Question.** Pose prompts that have multiple answers. For example, "How do we shine our lights in today's world?" You can make as many questions as desired.
2. **Whip Around.** "Whip" around the circle, calling on one student at a time. Have students share one of their responses. When called on, students should not repeat a response; they must add something new.
3. **Discuss.** After completing the whip around, have students discuss which ideas and themes showed up most in their responses.

Using the same "whiparound" process, students are only allowed to respond with one word and cannot write a list ahead of time. For example, you could give the prompt "plants and animals in the desert" and students respond quickly with the first answer that comes to their minds. You do not have to stop and correct students if they are wrong; simply go over those answers when the process is completed.

Closing Prayer: This is also the time for those who may want collective prayer for a situation.

Inter-Action!: *Create Your Own Talk Show:* Encourage your students to have fun, be creative, and shine.

www.ingramcontent.com/pod-product-compliance
Lightning Source LLC
Chambersburg PA
CBHW081728100526
44591CB00016B/2548